All-India Vegetarian Cookbook

A *Subzi Sutra*
containing the secrets of
India's multi-regional
vegetarian cuisine

All-India Vegetarian Cookbook

A *Subzi Sutra* containing the secrets of India's multi-regional vegetarian cuisine

Chef Zubin D'Souza
Corporate Chef

YBK Publishers
New York

YBK Publishers, Inc.
39 Crosby St.
New York, NY 10013
www.ybkpublishers.com

All-India Cookbook:
A *Subzi Sutra* Containing the Secrets of India's Multi-Regional Vegetarian Cuisine

ISBN: 978-0-9800508-9-9

Library of Congress Control Number: 2010920167

Manufactured in the United States of America,
or in the United Kingdom when distributed elsewhere.

Ver 10-01

This book is inspired by my son Zeus

One third of what we eat
keeps us alive,
the other two thirds
keeps the doctor alive

—Paramahansa Yogananda

Contents

The letter v to the left of a recipe's name indicates that it is vegan.

The letter v to the left of a recipe's name indicates that it is vegan.

The letter v to the left of a recipe's name indicates that it is vegan.

The letter v to the left of a recipe's name indicates that it is vegan.

The letter v to the left of a recipe's name indicates that it is vegan.

The letter v to the left of a recipe's name indicates that it is vegan.

The letter v to the left of a recipe's name indicates that it is vegan.

The letter v to the left of a recipe's name indicates that it is vegan.

The letter v to the left of a recipe's name indicates that it is vegan.

The letter v *to the left of a recipe's name indicates that it is vegan.*

A Brief Note From the Author

Living in India, one is surrounded by a population of more than seventy percent who profess belief in the necessity of a vegetarian diet. Not wishing to offend the religious sensitivities of your friends, one tends to join this observance, even if sometimes just half-heartedly.

What convinced me to go wholeheartedly vegetarian was the discovery that Alicia Silverstone followed these anti-carnivorous beliefs. I was young, a dreamer, and whatever in my spinach-fueled fantasies I pictured as the perfect date with her, I knew she would choose me if only I cooked for her the most memorable meal ever.

What began as a brief, meandering fantasia-like stroll turned into a voyage of epic proportion. I scouted all India seeking the most wonderful, the most innovative meals; the most satisfying, and sometimes the easiest to create in a jiffy (my fantasy was most imprecise as to how long our date would last).

I returned from this odyssey carrying many delicious recipes that I would as a chef develop further: scraps of paper; pencil-scribbled parchments; and twenty-two kilos—yes, fifty more pounds of pure pleasure that enhanced my waistline!

To take the trip was the best and most delicious decision I have ever made! Pleasing the palate is a wondrous and *pound*erous thing! The rest would be easy. All I would have to do is transcribe these wonderful foods to paper and cook them for her and, presto, I would win Alicia.

My little story, however, lacks the perfect ending. I still have not mustered the courage to call Alicia for that date of my dreams. If you are braver and more perseverant, and she accepts your invitation, please use this book to gain her heart. The recipes have been tried and tested to produce the same warming results each time. Eventually she will stumble across this book and realize that it is I, her Prince Valiant, who created the wonder in her palate. And, as is key in all fairy tales, we will live happily ever after.

Foreword

The recipes were collected by me from all over the Indian subcontinent. They are grouped by course—soup, starters, entrees and desserts. Main courses are grouped on the basis of their primary ingredient.

Most cookbooks follow the rule that ingredients appear in the recipe listed from top to bottom in the order in which they are used (added to the bowl). This rule has been followed in the main, barring the occasional exception. However, the primary ingredients of the dish are often mentioned first in my recipes. These are followed by the additional ingredients in the order in which they are added. This is done so that the reader easily sees what needs to be picked up on the next trip to the supermarket since I am assuming that you have already set up a basic Indian storehouse containing the most-used spices. This is discussed further on page 10.

Most of the recipes in this book have been calculated to serve four, and assuming that a single dish does not constitute an entire meal, it is anticipated that it will probably be served with another dish, condiments, and with rice or bread.

As you go through this cookbook and make discoveries, I would like you to tell me by email what they are. Like, say, what ingredients you find are absolutely necessary to your particular style of cooking; alterations you make that improve things; substitutions that improve; great resources you find in the U.S. for provisions or gadgets—anything at all you'd like to share with me. I will include your ideas with others and put them on my website

(http://www.chefzubin.com)

and, perhaps, include that idea (with credit to you, of course!) in an upcoming revised edition of the book. So write to me at zubin@chefzubin.com.

Throughout the book you will find website addresses for various uesful purposes. My publisher has gathered all those lengthy email addresses into one spot on the chefzubin website. When you find a website in the book that you'd like to go to, don't trouble yourself to copy the web address onto a piece of paper. Instead, go to www.chefzubin.com (don't forget to bookmark that address—you're going to want to go there a lot) and click the link on the first page that says "Links Mentioned in the Book." There you will find the addresses listed in this book. Click on each and you will be taken there.

My publisher plans to issue an inexpensive CD of the entire book. While it will mostly be a duplication of what's in the book, it will enable you to print the pages you will be cooking from. No need to flip the book over (into a small puddle of ghee) to keep it open and no need to turn pages back and forth between recipes. Pop the CD into your computer and print out pages 53, 67, 75, 107, and 201 and regale yourself and your guests with an amazing meal from soup to dumplings! If you insist on being traditional, print page 206 instead of page 201 and it will be soup to nuts. When you're done cooking throw those greasy pages away and then plan and print out your next meal. Write to me at zubin@chefzubin.com and I'll tell you how to get the CD.

And, while you're on the website, if you have any questions you'd like to ask me please feel free to write to me. You'll find another link there that says "Write to Zubin," so write to Zubin!. I promise to respond within a couple of days at the most. I want to hear how you like the book.; not so much that you don't, but I have strong shoulders, so you can even tell me that. Either way, I look forward to hearing from you.

Zubin D'Souza
January, 2010

Vegetarianism and the Vegan Diet

Although the concept of the vegetarian diet began in India around the second millennium, B.C.E., the term itself is a relatively recent invention. In 1847 the first vegetarian society was formed at Ramsgate in England. The originators borrowed their name from the Latin term vegetus which means "lively." The early society members claimed that their changed diet made them feel rejuvenated, energized and ready to take on the world.

Although this was the first registered society to open its membership to the public, the concept is by no means even a near modern invention. Pythagoras, the famed mathematician, and his followers embraced this ideal in the belief that so long as man destroyed defenseless creatures weaker than himself he would never enjoy peace or health.

Across the centuries many factors have led to the formation of branches of vegetarianism: veganism, fruitarianism, freeganism, flexitarianism—each with adherents who follow what they believe are ethically and morally sound beliefs.

Vegetarians, in the broad sense of the term, do not believe in eating the flesh of any animal.

Well, if you thought that you could be a vegetarian by eating only seafood (making you a pescatarian) you'd be wrong. The term is made quite precise, creating other terms of definition. Indians, who make up a majority of the vegetarian population of the world, are primarily lacto-vegetarians. They refrain from meat but follow a diet enriched with milk and dairy products.

Veganism is a much stricter form of vegetarianism. Vegans refrain from meat as well as such things as honey (because bees die during the collection process); milk and its by-products (because the calves and kids are deprived of their sustenance); and articles made of leather, silk, or wool.

Following is a list of some of the branches of vegetarianism and the basic outline of its form of belief.

Flexitarianism – This is close to the rules I follow to allow for my profession as a chef. It is a vegetarian diet that permits exceptions when the occasion demands it.

Freeganism—This is a modern diet often described as politically or world movement-inclined. Followers of this diet refrain from consuming anything that may promote capitalism, resorting to other earth-directed activities such as farming and foraging for their own food. While most freegans may follow the vegan path, they may sometimes choose to be flexible about consuming animal products they believe would otherwise be wasted while they will not contribute further to the ill-treatment meted out to animals.

Fruitarianism—This is a diet that consists of fruits, nuts, seeds, and edible plant matter that may be gathered without causing harm to the plant.

Lacto-ovo vegetarianism—This is a vegetarian diet allowing eggs or milk to provide necessary protein. Sometimes an adherent may choose only one of the two and is then termed an ovo-vegetarian or a lacto-vegetarian.

Pescatarianism—A diet that consists mainly of vegetarian food supplemented with seafood.

Pollotarianism—A diet that consists mainly of vegetarian food supplemented with chicken.

Raw veganism—A difficult diet followed by the ancient sages in India. It consists of raw fruits and berries, nuts, seeds, vegetables and sometimes flowers.

You, Indian Provisions, and the Internet

The average American cook, in reading through these recipes, is almost guaranteed to encounter one or more ingredients that he or she has never heard of. It is likely, too, that one will conclude that certain ingredients are available nowhere but in India. Not so! A good search term such as "Indian food products" plugged into Google will reveal a wealth of both local and buy-by-mail provisioners.

Need dried pomegranate seeds? Nothing is too esoteric that Google won't find it for you—about $4.00 for a lifetime supply, a 3-ounce jar. It will probably cost more than that to ship it to you, but think of the time you've saved shlepping around town, not finding it even at Esmerelda's Esoteric Edibles! So don't be put off by ingredients you may not be familiar with called for in this book. Sooner than you think, the package will be brought to you . Even fresh ingredients! They are flown in, often daily, just like strawberries from Chile.

Google is not put off by foreign language search terms. The Indian name for pomegranate seeds is anardana. Using the Indian term actually yields more and better "hits," websites at which one can purchase (in the U.S.) dried pomegranate seeds, than does using the English search term. Even better results are found by searching Google with "anardana seeds" as your search term. Anardana is available in other forms, such as powdered.

Placing a Google search term between double quotes in the search box will limit that search to the exact wording found within the quotes—including the words' order of appearance. Thus, you will not be presented with pumpkin, grass, bird feed, or a myriad of other seeds as you would if you do not put the term within quotes.

"I'm going to have to get a lot of stuff I never heard of." NOT TRUE!! You mostly already have what you'll need. Let me demonstrate with the ingredients list from the recipe for Bengali Stir-Fried Vegetables with Lentil Dumplings. I'm going to annotate each item with either "supermarket," if the item can be gotten there; "easy" if this is a specialty item that can be gotten at some upper end supermarkets in larger cities or in specialty food shops; "Asian" if findable at food shops that carry not just Indian foods; and, finally, Indian if it's likely to be found only at an Indian provisioner or by mail through the Internet.

From the supermarket (13 items):
Coriander seeds, ginger, bay leaf, dried red chilis, potato, eggplant, poppy seeds, milk, whole wheat flour, sugar, chili powder, and ghee (ghee is simply "drawn butter.")

From an upper-end supermarket (3 items):
White radish (daikon), plantain, snow peas

From Asian markets: (2 items)
mustard seeds, mustard oil

From an Indian provisioner (2 items):
Bori/sun dried lentil dumplings (optional).
Panch phoran.

(You can actually make panch phoran at home from items that will come straight out of your basic Indian spice closet. See page 10 for a discussion of the basic spices you will need and page 36 for the panch phoran recipe.)

I hope you'll agree that out of a total of 20 items needed for this recipe, two specialty items aren't many—especially since one is optional and the other you can make yourself!. By the way, I chose this recipe wholly at random. Other recipes will have a few items you might not have; most will not; for others, you'll have everything you need once you've got all the basics.

What's What

The table on the next few pages will help you find your ingredients either locally, through the Internet, or in Asian food stores. The table shows the Indian and English equivalent names for various ingredients

The naming of items, their transliteration from a language that uses a different letter set, can create confusion and prompts the same thing to be spelled in different ways. When an ingredient may have different names through usage, I try to point this out by direct reference or by simply using the names spelled in their different ways. Thus these may appear to be spelling errors, but they are, in fact, not.

It is a common bookmaking practice to italicize "foreign" words. As this book, though written in English, is acutally an Indian work, it does not treat Hindi and other Indian languages as foreign. Should I use a non English word that is not Indian, then it will be italicized. *Avanti!*

	HINDI	**ENGLISH**
MILK PRODUCTS	Paneer	Cheese
	Dahi	Yogurt
	ghee	Clarified butter
	Khoya	Reduced milk cakes
	Kheer	Rice pudding
CEREALS	Atta	Whole wheat flour
	Chawal	Rice
	Chawal atta	Rice flour
	Chira, poha	Flattened or beaten rice
	Maida	Refined wheat flour
	Moori, Murmura	Puffed rice (not to be confused with breakfast cereal)
	Seviyan	Vermicelli
	Ushna Chawal	Parboiled rice
	Sooji/Rawa	Semolina
LENTILS (DAL)	Toor/toovar dal	Split pigeon peas
	Besan	Chickpea flour
	Bori	Small sun dried cones of lentil paste
	Kabuli chana	Chickpeas, garbanzo beans
	Chana dal	Bengal gram (split chickpeas, without their seedcoat)
	Urad dal	Split black gram
	Matar dal	Yellow split peas
	Moong dal	Moong beans or green gram
	Masoor dal	Red lentil
	Papad	Poppadum
VEGETABLES	Aloo	Potato
	Bundh gobi	Cabbage
	Baigan	Brinjal/aubergine/eggplant
	Kancha kanthal	Green jackfruit
	Gajar	Carrot
	Turai	Ridged gourd
	Kacha kela	Green banana/plantain

	HINDI	**ENGLISH**
VEGETABLES (cont.)	Ghuiyan	Taro/arum root
	Karela	Bitter gourd, bitter melon
	Kaddu	Pumpkin
	Lauki	Bottle gourd, calabash
	Hara Matar	Green peas
	Kele-ka-phool	Banana blossom
	Mooli	Daikon/white radish
	Neem patti	Margosa leaves
	Suran	Elephant yam
	Paan	Betel leaf
	Palak	Spinach
	Gobi	Cauliflower
	Pyaz	Onion
	Pyaz patti	Scallions
	Parval/palwal	Pointed gourd
	Shakarkhand	Sweet potato
	Saag	Spinach
	Salgam	Turnip
	Kheera	Cucumber
	Seem/papdi	Broad bean
	Sarson-ka-saag	Mustard greens
	Kele-ki-tana	White pith of banana plant stem
FRUITS & NUTS	Aam	Mango
	Ananas	Pineapple
	Caju	Cashew
	Mungphalli	Peanut
	Phool Makhana	Lotus seed
	Kela	Banana
	Santra	Orange
	Keri/kacha aam	Unripe green mango
	Kanthal	Jackfruit
	Kismis	Raisin
	Ber	Indian plum

	HINDI	**ENGLISH**
FRUITS & NUTS (cont)	Nimbu	Lemon
	Nariyal	Coconut
	Papita	Papaya
	Pista	Pistachio
	Amrood	Guava
	Imli	Tamarind
BREADS	Kachori	Fried wheat pastry with seasoned filling
	Luchi/poori	Puffed fried flour bread
	Paratha	Thick crispy bread griddle fried in ghee
	Pau roti	Loaf of leavened bread
	Chapatti	Unleavened whole wheat flour bread
SPICES AND SEASONING	Adrak	Ginger
	Bada elaichi	Black cardamom
	Dalchini	Cinnamon
	Dhania	Coriander seeds
	Dhania patta	Cilantro/coriander leaves
	Elaichi	Green cardamom
	Garam Masala	A spice mixture of cinnamon, cardamom and cloves.
	Kala Mirch	Black pepper
	Haldi	Turmeric
	Hing	Asafoetida
	Zaffran	Saffron
	Jaiphal	Nutmeg
	Javitri	Mace
	Jeera	Cumin
	Ajwain	Carom seeds
	Kalonji	Black cumin, black onion seed
	Hara Mirch	Green chili
	Kari patta	Curry leaves
	Lavang	Cloves
	Saunf	Fennel
	Methi dana	Fenugreek seeds

	HINDI	ENGLISH
SPICES AND SEASONING (cont.)	Namak	Salt
	Khuskhus	Poppy seeds
	Pudina patti	Mint leaves
	Lasoon	Garlic
	Rai/Sarson	Mustard seeds
	Shahijeera	Aniseed
	Sukha lal mirch	Red dried chili
	Tej patta	Bay leaf
	Til	Sesame seed

The Indian Larder

So you think an Indian larder is too complicated to acquire and maintain? It ain't so!

One of the reasons people in the West often shy away from preparing Indian food is that they think an Indian grocery and spice list is difficult to obtain and too much to maintain. That is not the case as you already have much of it and the Internet can bring everything else to your door almost overnight—even to the flattest plain or prairie. While it may not yet be totally fleshed out (if you are reading this book soon after its publication) we have created a website that will provide up-to-date listings of places from which to order provisions. Have a look at http://www.chefzubin.com. If you can add to the list you find there please tell me your experiences in purchasing Indian products online by writing to me at zubin@chefzubin.com

Westerners think too that Indian cookery requires esoteric ingredients that are complicated and unavailable even beyond the complexity of its spicing. Not at all true. If you scan through the recipes in this book, the foundations of the majority of the dishes are things already in your kitchen: potatoes, onions, cauliflower, carrots, lentils, garbanzos, tomatoes, ginger, scallions—look for yourself and you'll find dozens more that you have in your kitchen right now, or you can find in your local supermarket. If you find this hard to believe, please see page 13 where I've broken down the entire book by its ingredients.

Indian food is not complicated. The versatility of its few basic spices and the lengthy existence of its cuisine has brought together basic ingredients, spicing, and methods that tend to complement each other in the overall, thus allowing one to constantly innovate and invent new flavor combinations. These combinations work simply because time has allowed this cuisine to learn its best ways of working together. This makes the need to stock a large array of spices unnecessary. Indian recipes, while they work perfectly when followed to the letter, are really just guides to Indian cookery.

I will lay out the basics of a reasonably stocked Indian kitchen. I have purposely not included ingredients that are probably already in the American kitchen.

Red chili powder Opt for the milder versions that are sold as 'Deghi Mirch'. This version is high on color and flavor but low on the heat scale. Such powders are great substitutes for fresh chilis or to pep up a mild curry that needs to be woken. Get different kinds, keep the ones that work best for you, and give the others to your cooking friends whose preferences are different from yours.

Turmeric is very versatile. It is used in almost all Indian meals for color and flavor and is a most valued spice among Indian cooks. Be sure to cook out the raw flavor completely as it can make a great tasting meal turn absolutely awful. However, turmeric burns easily, potentially spoiling a dish. Do not add it while roasting other spices, but cook it along with the main ingredients that provide moisture, protecting it from getting superheated.

Cumin seeds are unique in flavor, but familiar to the American palate in that it they are used in many international cuisines. They add great flavor to almost everything and it is one one of the spices that an Indian cook would absolutely have to take to the proverbial desert island.

Cinnamon, cardamom, clove this whole-spice trio adds instant flavor and appeal to standard favorites such as biryanis and stews.

Mustard seeds These add a tinge of sharpness to the dish. Always add only a pinch because an excess of these seeds can make the final product somewhat bitter.

Dried red chillies These are used in a variety of ways as shown in the recipes. In their simplest use, they can be pounded in a mortar and pestle into coarse chili flakes that will spice up any mild dish.

Tamarind Available in the form of cakes, paste, pulp or whole, it adds sourness and an entirely new dimension to the dish.

What Do You *Really* Need?

What spices and staples should you always keep on hand?

Counting on my fingers and toes, I found the following information:

Turmeric is used in 81 recipes. Green cardamom is used in 42 recipes. Based on their occurence in recipes, following are the items you should keep replenished and always at hand. Following this guide, it is most likely that you will then have all you need to cook many of the recipes in this book.

Spices

Turmeric	Green cardamom	Dried red chilis
Chili powder	Coriander seeds	Cumin seeds
Mustard oil	Mustard seeds	

Staples

Green chilis	Coriander leaves (cilantro)	Garlic
Ginger	Onions	Potatoes
Tomatoes		

What If I Want to Have Everything?

Switching from counting on my fingers and toes, I needed a scientific calculator to help me to list every ingredient needed to cook evey recipe in this book. While this information is not very useful for cooking the recipes, there are those among you who think that Indian food ingredients are exotic and hard to find. Scanning this list will prove otherwise to you. They're listed alpahbetically, not by how often they are needed:

Spices

Asofetida
Baking soda
Bay leaf
Black rock salt
Cardamom, green
Cardamom, black
Carom seeds
Chaat masala
Chilis, dried red
Chili powder
Cinnamon
Cloves
Coconut oil
Copra
Coriander seeds
Coriander powder

Cumin seeds
Cumin powder
Curry leaves
Drumstick
Fennel seeds
Fenugreek seeds
Fenugreek leaves
Garam masala
Ginger, powdered
Malt vinegar
Mango powder
Mace
Mint leaves
Mustard oil
Nustard seeds
Neem leaves

Nigella
Nutmeg
Panch phoran (see page 36)
Papads (pappadum)
Peanuts
Peppercorns
Pomegranate seeds
Rosewater
Saffron
Sesame oil
Sesame powder
Sesame seeds
Star anise
Tamarind
Turmeric
Yellow mustard seeds

Staples

Almonds
Apples
Beets

Bitter melon
Broad beans
Cabbage

Carrots
Cashews
Cauliflower

Chilis

Coconut milk

Coconut, fresh, dessicat-
ed, or dried

Condensed milk

Coriander (cilantro)

Corn meal

Corn starch

Cream

Cucumber

Daikon

Dates

Eggplant

Flour, white

Flour, whole wheat

Flour, chick pea

Garlic

Ghee

Ginger

Green peppers

Honey

Lemon

Lentils

Lime

Mango

Milk

Mushroom

Onions

Paneer

Papaya

Peas

Pistachio

Pineapple

Plantain

Potato

Pumpkin

Pumpkin, white

Raisins

Rice

Rice flour

Rose petals

Scallion

Semolina

Shallot

Spinach

Snow peas

Soya nuggets

String beans

Tomatoes

Vinegar

Yams

Yeast

Yogurt

So, if you're the kind of person who has to have every last little thing on hand before feeling ready to cook, there it is! You'll find this list on my website, www.chefzubin.com. Print it out, go to the supermarket, stop by your local Indian provisioner and buy every one of these things. Then pop your mortar and pestle onto the counter and COOK!!!

Spices

Spices grown in India are stronger in flavor than American equivalents. Use them sparingly when a pinch is called for because they are meant to lightly flavor the dish and not to overpower it—but you will have to use more of the American variety to achieve the same result. Do not overdo, as unexpectedly chewing a bunch of crunchy spices is sometimes not a pleasant sensation.

Indians may speak in generality about how one must "roast the spices before grinding them to a powder." This is a very important step in extracting the best potential flavor from a spice.

Its distinctive flavor and fragrance has literally to be coaxed out of the spice by applying heat to it. Many spices do not have a pleasant taste or aroma in their raw form. If one were simply to grind a collection of raw spices into a powder, raw bitterness and resin-like flavor would be conveyed to the dish. Roasting the spices (as explained on Page 39) prevents this by converting that rawness to wonderful flavor and beautiful aroma.

In roasting spices prior to grinding them, use a dry hot pan. Roast each spice individually because, if roasted together, some may burn before the others have had a chance to change color and release their flavor and aroma.

Spices may release their flavor in other methods than the dry roasting process, all involving heat. This can be done by simmering them in sauces or by super-heating them in hot oil so that the heat splits them open.

Heat is the crucial factor in the process. Spices such as mustard, if started in cold oil, will absorb the oil and refuse to split. This will give an unpleasant bitter taste to the dish.

Cumin/Jeera is a member of the parsley family. It is a pretty plant that sprouts clusters of white and pink flowers. The seeds are used to season food. It is normally found in three colors: white, black, and amber. The black seeds are the ones most commonly used.

Cardamom pods/Chota elaichi come from a perennial bush that is normally between six and ten feet high. It is highly valued for its rich fragrance and distinctive flavor. It is among the most expensive spices in the world, partly because each pod must be hand harvested.

Fenugreek/Methi seeds are known throughout India, but this spice's popularity has not travelled very much. It is used extensively in Bengali and South Indian cuisine.

Methi seeds are small, hard, and straw-colored. They impart a nutty flavor with a bitter undertone. They should not be used in excess as they can make the dish very bitter.

The Fenugreek plant provides us with wonderfully edible leaves and shoots. They are used in a wide variety of Indian food preparations from salads to sweets.

Curry leaves/kadi patta — The English word curry comes from a misreading and shortening of the native name of these leaves, kariveppilai. They may be used fresh or dried. A traditional home on the countryside will have a curry leaf tree in the back yard to provide an unending fresh supply of this wonderful flavor.

Curry leaves are used widely in the cuisines of southern India. They provide a fresh zesty fragrance and a mild astringency to the food. They can be found at many Indian provision stores in the U.S. and will keep well under refrigeration for a couple of months. Even though the leaves will tend to dry out while under prolonged refrigeration, there is no perceptible loss of fragrance or flavor when they are finally used. If you just can't find them anywhere, then simply omit them from the recipe as there is really no comparative substitute. The dish will note its absence, but the overall flavor will not be altered negatively.

When using curry leaves, you can use just the leaves or the leaves with its stalk. If you retain the stalk, you should remove and discard all at the end of cooking as the flavor will have been imparted to the dish. If you've used the leaves alone they will soften enough to become incorporated into the dish.

Carom seeds/bishop's weed/ajwain resembles a smaller version of caraway seeds. It has a unique sharp and pungent flavor. It is normally used in Indian food to brighten the flavor of certain kinds of dough and bland vegetables.

Black cardamom pods/badi elaichi are distinctly different from the fragrant green pods cited earlier. They are mostly used with other spices to create a garam masala mix (a recipe is provided on page 49). It can be used whole to season lamb curries and to flavor some sweetmeats.

Asafoetida/hing is a gummy, resin-like substance that is secreted by the dill plant. It is available in powdered or whole (stiff jelly-like) form. It imparts a strong, almost sulphurous fragrance. (If using the whole form, dissolve it in a bit of warm water beforehand.)

Coriander seeds/coriander leaves/Dhaniya Coriander seeds are grouped under spices and the leaves fall under herbs. They have separately distinct fragrances and flavors. Coriander leaves are better known in the U.S. as cilantro.

Fennel seeds/Saunf Although the fennel bulb is rarely found in Indian cooking, the seeds figure prominently. Along with other uses, fennel seeds are used to lend fragrance to some desserts.

Turmeric/Haldi This rhizome is cultivated in most parts of India and is one of the most widely used spices in Indian cooking. It is used in almost every preparation and in every regional cuisine.

Black peppercorns/kali mirch are grown mostly in Kerala. At one time they were very expensive—worth almost their weight in gold. In the past, part of a worker's wages was paid with cloves and peppercorns.

Dried mango powder/Amchoor is made by sun-drying pieces of raw mango and grinding them to a powder. Salt is used during the drying process, so the resulting powder is normally a bit salty. Sprinkling this on finished kebabs or on salads provides a tang that is very pleasant.

Mustard seeds/Rai or Sarson Mustard seeds, mustard oil, and mustard leaves are used in several parts of India. Mustard has a very sharp, strong, and acidic flavor and fragrance. The seeds are available in three varieties: smaller black, larger (and milder) brown, and yellow.

Saffron/Zaffran/Kesar This is hands-down the most expensive flavoring in the world. Saffron strands are the stamens of the crocus flower. Each saffron strand is individually hand picked. Saffron imparts a beautiful orange color when dissolved. Dissolving it in a bit of milk before use gives the best results. The lactic acid in the milk helps to release the flavor.

Cloves/Laung Along with black peppercorns, these were the spices most in demand in ancient times. Wars were fought to establish control of the shipping routes to South India for the trade in spices. Cloves provide a sharp, astringent flavor.

Poppy seeds/Khus khus Poppy seeds impart a distinct nutty taste to food. They are soaked in water before being ground into a paste. The raw flavor should be cooked out before it is used. This occurs when the paste is added during cooking.

Cinnamon is the product of an evergreen tree that belongs to the family Lauraceae. It originally grew in Sri Lanka (formerly Ceylon), and was a secret protected by many generations of merchants and spice traders to control their interests and monopoly in this spice. Cinnamon is not to be confused with the milder flavored cassia bark that originated in China.

Cinnamon has a characteristically sweet fragrance that it imparts to a preparation. When called for in the recipes in this book, the pieces should be about two inches long.

Chaat Masala As the name masala suggests, this is a tangy mixture that is a combination of spices and dried mango powder. It is sprinkled over kebabs, chaats and salads and is sometimes sprinkled on fruits or fruit salads to add a savory zing. (A recipe is provided on p. 49.)

Dried Chilis/Sukha Lal Mirch are available all over India; they range in strength (or "heat") from mild Kashmiri chilis to seriously challenging Naga chilis. They are ground to flakes for sprinkling or into a fine powder to season food.

In India dried chilis are always red. In the U.S. one finds poblanos or achiotes, and other chilis, that are black.

Green chilis/Hari mirch Like the red, sun-dried versions, these chilis, too, range from mild, barely perceptible, to scorching. (A discussion of chilis follows.)

Bengali Five Spice/Panch Phoran See recipe and discussion on page 36.

Chilis

Yes!—one inevitably comes to the question of chilis!

Chilis of quite differing kinds are grown all over the world. Indians grow several thousand varieties for domestic consumption as well as for export. So how are we to decide on the type of chili we should use to give the best result?

Before I answer that, let us have a brief history of this much loved and sometimes wisely feared fruit.

The chili is believed to have originated in South or Central America between 5,000 B.C.E. and 3,400 B.C.E. They were originally used as weapons. Dried and powdered it was thrown at an enemy. It is still occasionally used in India and elsewhere by a variety of bag-snatchers and other low lifes. The use of chilis may be the earliest recorded version of chemical warfare on the planet.

As early as about 2,000 B.C.E., archaeological evidence confirms the use of chilis in food in the western hemisphere. Columbus brought chilis back to Europe, referring to them as red peppers, an image that has held to this day. With the rise in maritime power of Spain and Portugal and their frequent trips to the Americas—stopping off in Africa for fresh water, supplies, and all the slaves they could carry—the spread of chilis across most of the known world was accomplished in the short span of about fifty years.

When the Portuguese landed at Goa in India, they brought with them several species of exotic plants from the new world. Along with breadfruit and potatoes were several varieties of chilis that were planted in the fertile Goan soil. From then on, merchants, travelers, and invading armies helped to distribute chilis all over India.

Although the chilis in India originated with the same chilis used in the cuisine of the Americas, the soil differences and climatic conditions have helped each variety to evolve individual characteristics in flavor and spiciness.

The basic rules for the use of chilis in cookery are simple enough.

    —the smaller the fruit, the spicier it tends to be.

    —removing the seeds helps reduce the heat level of the chili.

Many will contend otherwise, but in Indian cooking it does not matter which variety of chili is used. Indian cooking relies on a blend of spices for flavor, not on the chili. The chili plays only a supporting role by adding heat, that heat varying according to the type of chili used.

Most of my recipes refer to green chilis, which is the only variety of fresh chilis available in Indian markets. These long green chilis are commonly available in the United States. Using a fresh red chili instead of a green one will make no difference in the final outcome.

Fresh red chilis are generally not available in the U.S. They are simply ripened green chilis.

Dried red chilis are much used in Indian cuisine. They are often quick-roasted in a pan with hot oil or are steeped in vinegar for twenty minutes to release their flavor before being ground to a paste.

When a recipe calls for red chili paste, I find that the best way forward is to boil dried red chilies in a bit of water for a minute and then simmer them for ten more minutes before grinding them to a paste.

A few recipes are chili-specific (some pickles and chutneys), but in most recipes, the variety of chili used is immaterial. I am sometimes pressed to be definitive about the type of chili to be used in a given recipe, but I recommend that one rely on one's own taste and preferences as to the introduction of heat.

There are perhaps four levels of heat, which we might call mild, medium, hot, and call 911! Your provisioner will help you to identify the heat level of the chilis it sells. If you're not familiar with a given variety do not hesitate to ask about it. If you don't, your family members or guests may not speak to you for the entire evening due to temporary laryngeal paralysis. (In some cases this may be a good thing.)

Some recipes call for chopped chilis; some for slit chilis (defined below); some for dried chilis. Any and each can be substituted for any other. If the recipe calls for a chili known to be quite hot and your preference is for mild, use the milder chili you prefer.

Residents of certain provinces in India are partial to their locally grown varieties and may even claim the ability to tell them from poorer flavored relatives. This claim is true enough as many of the native population enjoy fresh chilis eaten raw during the meal just as someone might choose a carrot stick.

The spread of chilis throughout the cuisine of India came more out of economic necessity than a cultural or food-related need. With the opening of new geographies and new trade routes, the demand for, and consequently the price of spices climbed higher, putting them out of reach of the poorer segments of society.

Chilis, a cheaper alternative than more expensive spices, put the zing back into the Indian's curry. It was also found that eating a lot of chilis prompted the drinking of much water to calm the burning feeling. This provided both an oral taste sensation as well as that the water filled them, providing a feeling of satiation in spite of the meagerness of their rations.

Removing the seeds and chopping the chilis will reduce the heat—but chopping the chilis also carries the danger of an unsuspecting guest biting into a chunk. Slit green chilis are perhaps a better alternative. Leave the head and the stem on the chili. Make a lengthwise slit in the flesh, (into the hollow of the chili, but not so deep as to release many seeds) and put it into the pot whole. This releases the flavor while leaving the chili available to be removed before serving.

Your experience will soon dictate the kind and amount of chilis that appeals to your palate. Moreover, it is certain that over time your palate will change—probably toward more, rather than less, heat.

The recipes in this book are moderately to mildly spiced. Enough chilis are added as to give you a good representation of how it is prepared traditionally, but restrained enough to ensure that hospitalization should not be necessary.

I want to hear from readers about the kinds of chilis you use and how you prepare them. I will try to compile this into a U.S. guide that will appear later on the website we are building (http://www.chefzubin.com) and incorporate it into a later printed edition. Send your email to me at zubin@chefzubin.com.

Of Fats and Oils

Because Indians tend to eat a lot of vegetarian food, they use a great deal of ghee (clarified butter) and oil to compensate for the lack of meat in their regimen.

The use of copious amounts of oil and fat had been linked to status—the more you used, the higher you were on the social ladder. Now that modern discoveries have led people to being more health conscious this has mostly eliminated the social advantage of flaunting one's oily excesses.

I remember as a child, being invited to a marriage feast during which the host family publicly berated the poor caterer for not having at least four inches of oil floating on the surface of the curry. (This was a general practice for which the original measure was a member of the groom's family who would check the food before it was served to the guests. He would place the back of his palm against the pot and determine whether the oil slick reached above the height of four of his chubby fingers.) One had to stir away the oil slick before discovering what kind of curry there was beneath.

Recently, olive oil has begun to be used in some Indian homes, but its flavor tends to stick out from the background of the dish.

Of the various types of oils that Indians use, I personally find sunflower oil to be my favorite. It has a flavor that is almost unnoticeable and it blends in well with the rest of the dish.

Ground nut oil is high in cholesterol and has a quite distinct, even overpowering flavor and fragrance.

Ayurveda is an ancient Indian medical science that originated about five thousand years ago. The word means the 'Science of Life' in Sanskrit. The basic belief of Ayurveda is that each person possesses a unique body and constitution and that most illnesses originate from a diet or lifestyle that is not in sync with the requirements of that unique body. This science was discovered and propagated by Indian monks and sages who carried out extensive research into the properties of various food ingredients and their effects on the individual constitution. This science, which is still practiced, extols the virtues of a tailor made diet that follows ayurvedic principles.

Ayurveda dwells at length on the subject of oils. Various oils such as linseed (Americans know this as flaxseed oil. When called linseed oil it is an inedible version that is used to thin oil-based paint.), safflower, sesame, coconut, mustard, sunflower and cottonseed oils, along with ghee (clarified butter) have been studied. According to Ayurveda the different types of fats or oils should be consumed in a one third ratio. According to this belief, a perfect combination for cooking would be a blend of one-third saturated fatty acids like ghee or butter, one-third of Omega3 oils like mustard and a third of Omega6 oils like sesame or coconut. Among the oils, sesame has been declared the leader by far due to the nutrition it provides and the taste it adds.

Though several Vedic teachings mention that ghee is a most beneficial product for your body, they also caution about the ill effects of using too much of any substance.

Mustard oil is used mainly in the East of India, in the states of Bengal, Orissa, Bihar, Madhya Pradesh and certain parts of Uttar Pradesh. It is a healthy alternative choice, but has a strong sulphurous fragrance.

Most of the coastal areas use coconut oil, which is readily available and has great flavor, but the people there tend to overdo its use, inevitably leading them to obesity. According to ancient writings, coconut oil, if used in moderation, is beneficial to one's health.

Oil is required in the diet. It really should not matter what kind of oil is used so long as it is restricted to that amount that is the minimum level required. Many of the recipes in this book call for oil to make them vegan friendly. However, one can use an equal amount of ghee instead.

Most Indian recipes use oils rather than ghee in which to fry. This is due to its high cost, but frying in ghee results in a longer lasting crispness than does the use of other oils.

Ghee

In India, there is a folk saying that translates to suggest that ghee will provide one with more benefit than one's parents and the entire medical practice put together.

Ghee has a long and illustrious history. Butter, from which ghee is made, is thought to have been discovered by nomadic herdsmen galloping their horses while carrying bags of milk, thus churning the cream into lumps of butter.

Ghee holds a position of great significance in the Ayurveda, the ancient Indian natural medical system that is still practiced today. Ghee, clarified butter, has made its way into several sacred Vedic texts and hymns including the famous Mahabharata. It is used as a sacrifice during several Hindu ceremonies and is considered by the Hindus to be one fifth of the substance that gave the gods their immortality.

Ghee is pure fat. It is butter that has had its nonfat milk solids and water removed. It has a shelf life that far outlasts butter and can be stored in an airtight container for a few months without refrigeration. It is a product available in many supermarkets and at all Indian provision stores around the globe and can easily be prepared at home as well.

When prepared in the traditional manner ghee starts with home-churned butter. Worth searching for and difficult to procure, ghee simmered in clay pots over a wood fire gives a beautiful smokiness to the product. Its fragrance is ethereal, and makes a real difference in a finished dish. However, this smoked version is usually made by farmers for their own consumption and they become near-violent should you try to make off with their precious store. I suggest you settle for the conventional unless you are lucky enough to discover a good approximation available commercially.

Having escaped the farmer, it's safer to make one's own ghee.

The microwave method is easiest. Place a pound of unsalted butter in a deep dish and cover it with something non-metallic. As microwave devices are notoriously variable as to their heat production, start with a medium setting (or less) which should be high enough to ensure that the water evaporates from the liquid and the fat separates from the milk solids, coming to rest at the bottom. Gently spoon or pour off and reserve the clear golden liquid at the top so as to not disturb the solids at the bottom. This is lovely ghee. Store it in an airtight container, unrefrigerated.

The pan method requires a bit of patience and practice. Place a pound of soft, unsalted butter in a thick-bottomed pan and gently simmer it for about ten minutes until the liquid comes to heat and begins to froth. Increase the heat gradually so that the liquid bubbles. Immediately reduce to a simmer again. Skim off the froth that rises to the top. When the surface liquid appears clear and you see flecks of solids at the bottom it is ghee. Remove from the heat and spoon or pour off the ghee carefully to avoid mixing in the solids.

When ghee is called for in a recipe, an equal amount of butter may be substituted if one bears in mind that butter will burn at a low temperature, while ghee's smoke point is higher, even, than vegetable oils. It is the milk solids in the butter (removed during clarification) that burn.

When a tiny amount of oil, even a drop, is added to butter heating in a pan, it significantly raises the temperature at which the butter will begin to brown and burn. Will the chemists among you please tell me why this is so? Write to me at zubin@chefzubin.com and we'll post your answer on our website and include your explanation in the next edition of the *All-India Vegetarian Cookbook* with attribution to you, of course.

Rice

Ever since the first rice grains were grown on earth, they have been a source of sustenance, succor, and even an enigma to humankind. Rice has variously been described in ancient mythologies as a boon from the gods to a gift from the earth to thank men for their labors. It has had several mentions in ancient Vedic texts, in medical treatises like the Sushrutha Samitha and in the Charaka Samitha and has even had its virtues carved into the ancient Pramban temples of Java.

When rice became a farmed crop more than six thousand years ago, there would have been few to realize that this grain would rise to such prominence as to command armies and alter conquests, influence foreign policy, and to broadly affect the lifestyle and the eating habits of more than half of the world's population.

Among Indians, rice also holds quasi religious importance. Rice is used in several religious ceremonies to indicate prosperity and to appease several deities. Babies go through a religious ceremony denoting their move to solid foods and are fed rice as part of their first meal. Newlyweds are showered with rice grains to promote fertility. (This is less done in the U.S. since it was discovered that eating uncooked rice is harmful to birds.)

The reason that rice came to such great use is because of its amazing ability to grow in various terrains, but that it is especially suited to the wet, long monsoon season that most areas of South-east Asia endure. Rice farming and its harvesting is heavily labor intensive and the reason why its cultivation has not spread across the globe beyond its agrarian roots.

In India, where thousands of varieties of rice are grown, Basmati rice is proclaimed supreme. This is not because it is in fact so superior a strain of the grain, but due to a subtle and well-played marketing policy.

When the Mughal Empire overran most of the central and northwest portion of the sub-continent, they demanded tithes and tributes. Rice was a crop that was available in plenty and plans were put in place by the rulers of some smaller principalities to lessen their taxation. Above the others, Basmati rice was touted as a gift from the gods. Poets waxed lyrically about it and story tellers carried great tales of Basmati woven with excitement and adventure wherever they went.

Sure enough, the rice was soon invested with such great value that it became one of the tributes required to be laid before the royal thrones.

Not that Basmati is overstated as to its goodness. It is a wonderful long-grained rice with subtle fragrance and its lower starch content promotes less stickiness and easier-to-achieve kernel separation.

The use of a particular strain of rice in Indian cooking has more to do with economic and regional factors than those of taste. Basmati has always been a premium rice and is therefore used for celebration feasts. On the other hand, Bengalis swear by their short-grained, locally grown Gobindobhog, a strain of rice that remains unknown to most outside of their region. Farmers living in rural communities often eat healthier unpolished rice, with only the husk removed, the more expensive milled rice being sold to city dwellers who can afford the additional processing charges.

The harvesting of rice is done mainly by hand. The kernels are hulled with a machine called a rice huller that strips off the outer husks of the grain. At this stage, what is called brown rice is perhaps one of the healthiest grains to eat. The grains are further milled to polish off the bran and turn them into eye-pleasing pearly white grains. Often these grains are rolled in powdered starch to give them a shiny appearance.

Parboiled rice which is often used in the villages that dot the Indian landscape is more nutritious than milled rice and almost equal (about 80%) in nutrition to brown rice. The parboiling process takes place before milling and transfers the nutrients into the grain itself. Sold in the U.S., "Uncle Ben's" is parboiled rice.

Rice must be rinsed several times before cooking to remove all traces of starch. This enhances kernel separation as the starch acts as a glue. (This rule does not apply to fortified varieties of rice that warn that rinsing results in the loss of added nutrients.)

The two most common methods of preparing rice are the steaming method and the boiling method. (A "cooking" variation is the practice by raw vegans and fruitarians who sprout the grains and consume the grass, a process that takes about a fortnight.)

Electric rice cookers have eliminated much of the stress and overcooking previously associated with the steaming method. The rice begins in an excess of water that both steams off and is absorbed into the kernels, rendering them soft yet chewy. The traditional method is to simmer the grains in twice their amount of salted water until all the liquid has been absorbed and the rice grains become fluffy.

Not often used in the U.S., the boiling method is used by most Indians. Much-rinsed rice is put into ten times its amount of salted, boiling water, cooking it much like one would cook pasta. The grains, depending on their type, should take from twelve to fifteen minutes to soften (or less—cooking should be stopped when sampling a few kernels indicates they are done). The rice is then strained.

Many marvel at the rice served in Indian restaurants as the kernels are invariably individual, dry—almost never clumped How do they accomplish this? First, they use long-grained varieties of rice like basmati. It must be rinsed multiple times, until the water runs clear. Then it is cooked in many times the amount of boiling water as rice, minmally four times, more is better, adding a teaspoon of oil or ghee for each quart of water used. Keep at moderate boil, stirring lightly, occasionally, to move rice and oil around. When cooked through, perhaps less than ten minutes (stop immediately when sampling a few kernels indicates they are done) drain in a colander after rinsing it liberally once more under the tap to stop cooking and to eliminate further starch. Tossing the colander lightly (to not break the kernels) while the rice is draining will get more of the water out. Then spread the rice on a tray to dry as the rice draws water back into itself. Key is the rinsing! Spreading on a tray helps, but multiple rinsing, before and, again, after cooking, is the answer. Rice can be dished out at room temperature as the heat from the other dishes served with it will quickly reheat it. Or, a few seconds in the microwave will bring it to heat.

Rice being a neutrally flavored grain, it tends to absorb and enhance the flavor of the ingredients that it associates with. This attribute enables equally the subtle flavoring of rice, as in a pilaf, as well as when it is served with a powerfully flavorsome curry.

Adding whole spices like cardamom, cinnamon and cloves to the water while boiling or steaming the rice tends to enhance its taste.

While many of my recipes call for Basmati rice you may substitute with any style of rice that you like. It should be noted that the quantity of water needed for steaming will vary according to the type of rice being prepared. Experimentation will soon reveal the correct amount.

The Thali and Other Conventions of Eating "Indian Style"

India is a land of great contrast. There are vast swaths of arid desert contrasted with lush farmland; past and present majestic palaces counter present-day slums; fertile valleys, polluted cities, mountains, beaches. You get the point. India is a large land of large contrasts.

These contrasts have manifested themselves into the tradition and understanding of its peoples, creating a kaleidoscope of culinary method steeped with ancient custom that unifies the whole.

It is said that each twenty kilometers (about a dozen miles) of travel brings one to a new presiding deity, a different dialect, and an entirely new twist to the cuisine. The thali enables one to include all these characteristics into one meal.

But before we come to the serving characteristics of the meal, I would like to point out some of the tradition about eating. Every meal is considered a celebration of life and a reason to thank the heavens for their bounty. As the majority of the nation tends to be somewhat spiritual in many aspects of their lives, they add a dash during meal times as well.

Before the meal, the males in the family ensure that they have washed their hands and feet well. They sit in a single straight line with their plates or banana leaves before them. They symbolically sprinkle a bit of water in a circle around themselves to purify the area and sprinkle a bit more on their plates and wipe it off with a napkin.

Many of these dining traditions continue in rural India, while the space and time constraints imposed on urban areas has pretty much erased the possibility of clinging to these ancient ways.

However, most Hindus, irrespective of their location continue to sprinkle water around their plates to create the sacred purified circle. Sitting in a straight line and the use of the banana leaf as a plate is now restricted to the villages.

The women of the family begin to serve the food, each carrying a component of the meal. The first to be served is the eldest male and the serving proceeds further according to one's age and status within the family. In rural areas, where several generations of a family may live together under one roof, this may be more than twenty men. All of the food is served at once. Each serving of a separate dish is designated its own specific zone on the plate or leaf—the concept of the thali.

This ordering of status is dictated within a structure known legally in India as HUF or Hindu Undivided Family (also Hindu Joint Family). Status begins with the eldest male, moves to the eldest son, and so on. The eldest male is known as the 'Karta Purush' who makes all business decisions including the decisions of marriage alliances, and the appropriate education of the siblings and grand children. Women are intentionally kept out of the decision-making sphere, they being relegated to domestic duties.

Viewing this system from the inside I can tell you that the system works. I just wish I could implement it at my house! My wife, Shraboni has turned out to be the Karta Purush!!! I'm guessing that were I to rigorously attempt to enforce this code of society in my own household I would likely be wearing my filled banana leaf inverted as a hat!

For those among you who would like to learn more about the Hindu Joint Family, Wikepedia has a very informative article under that name.

When the men have completed their meal, the banana leaves are rolled up and fed to the cattle. They leave the dining room to leave the women to serve their own meal. Today, in an age of gender-equality and modernization, this process has been greatly streamlined resulting in what is widely known as the all-encompassing thali.

Although many claim that the thali (the concept of compartmentalization) was devised in the state of Gujarat, which lies on the Western coast, it has existed in various manners all across the nation and only its present form, the metal compartmented dish, came from Gujarat.

The thali derives its name from the word thaal which simply means a metal plate or platter. The components of a thali are the plate and several metal bowls which rest upon it, usually six, allowing separated portions to be provided to each person partaking in the meal.

Ringed by the bowls, a mound of rice is placed in the center of the thali. In each of the bowls is placed one of the components of the meal, varying by the preparations of the day—a raita, perhaps, a simple salad, a rasam or shorba, a lentil preparation (dal), a vegetable curry or, perhaps, some greens and a potato preparation.

While many Americans don't seem to realize it, Indians eat a lot of salads. It's just that we don't often use lettuce because India's heat doesn't permit its easy growth. The simplest Indian salad is a mix of onions, tomatoes, cucumber, chilies, lemon juice, and salt. You'll find a number of salad recipes in this book.

Special occasions may call for a paneer dish to be prepared to replace one of those more regularly served. Pickles and chutneys and, often, roasted papads (usually referred to in U.S. restaurants as pappadum) may be placed on the plate near the rice.

The objective in using the thali is to convey to the diner a taste of the variety of flavors and textures that are an important part of any Indian meal—an Indian tasting menu, so to speak. Often the meal will include homemade unleavened breads, or rotis. Many Indians love having both rice and bread with each meal.

While a thali may seem a bit ostentatious and something of a waste of time to so carefully compartmentalize, it just isn't that. Most of the foods are simple regular fare created with quick basic preparations which, when presented together on the thali, make a meal what it was originally meant to be—a celebration!

Americans who eat out regularly at Indian restaurants will have discovered that Indian food complements Indian food—that various dishes can be mixed together to achieve different flavor results that are most delicious together—an advantage of the thali, where everything is on one plate.

Basic Kitchen Equipment

Though the preparation of most Indian meals does not require special equipment, a collection of a few of the items discussed in this section will definitely help to facilitate your procedures. Indeed, many kitchens will already contain many of them.

Part of a chef's training is to be asked the hypothetical question, "What would you take with you to be stranded on a deserted island?" Apart from my inevitable and immediate first answer—Alicia Silverstone (with Natalie Portman running a close second)—I've come up with a brief list of devices that are near necessities.

Food Processor This is one of those basic machines that every kitchen should have for any kind of cookery. Many Indian recipes call for ground pastes or ground spices. You can find basic grinders right up to more complicated electric all-in-one food processing units. While some of the recipes suggest grinding spices in a food processor, small amounts of spices will get lost in and not be properly ground in a full-sized processor. A smaller processor or a spice grinder will do better.

Muscle is sometimes an issue. Grinding pastes in a simple home bar blender can place an immense strain on the motor causing it to burn out Also there is the residual effect as well—cardamom martini anyone? An effective and efficient alternative (with the added benefit of healthful exercise) is the simple mortar and pestle.

Mortar and pestle This is a great piece of kitchen equipment that manages to simultaneously replace the food processor and a visit to the gym. Taking every opportunity to be green, several energy conservationists I know totally reject the motorized practicality of food processors in favor of the mortar and pestle. I prefer those made of stone to the lighter wooden versions. Stone washes off easier and does not absorb flavors as wood will.

Thick-bottomed pot/Handi Many of my recipes call for the use of a thick-bottomed pot. The purpose of the thick bottom is that Indian food is often simmered or stewed for long periods of time. There is greater chance for the spices to stick to the bottom and burn. To minimize this, use a thick-bottomed pot; it distributes the heat more evenly and lessens heat concentration at the center of the pot. A short, squat pot with a mouth slightly wider than its base is preferable to the tall and slimmer stockpot types.

Heavy, round-bottomed wok/Kadhai This is a versatile item in Indian culinary preparation. They are filled with oil for deep-frying food. Thinner versions are used for rapid stir-frying while heavier ones made of thicker metal are used to prepare vegetable stews and curries.

Deep sauté pan This is a piece of equipment that pleases me for its multi-functionality. The high sidewalls and flat surface make it admirably suited to preparing small quantities of curry, can be filled with oil to replicate a deep-fat fryer, and can be used to dry-roast spices before grinding them.

Griddle plate or griddle pan/Tava With so many advances in technology, grandma's original cast-iron pans have been almost replaced, but I understand that, among devotees, such a statement is almost irreligious. Griddles are perfect for baking unleavened bread, sear-frying kebabs and cutlets, and do a pretty good job of replicating the baking normally resultant of a tandoor oven.

Rolling Pin This is a true necessity if breads are going to be a part of your meal. It's probable that your kitchen already has one and it's likely to be wooden; most Indians prefer the wooden ones. When rolling out a dozen or more breads all you need is a sturdy pin that is comfortable for you to use. Heavier rolling pins do a good job of crushing spices and cracking nuts as well.

* * *

Note: Indian food processors have a special attachment, a tiny jar, like a coffee grinder, with which we grind our spices. I've checked and found that these attachments are not easily available in the U.S. (American importers, take note!) If a fortunate reader should happen upon an equivalent device available in the U.S., please let our other readers know this by writing to me at zubin@chefzubin.com. I will pass the word along on our website: www.chefzubin.com.

Basic Preparations

While I expect that many readers will be familiar with cookery in general and the basic preparations required for Indian cooking, there are those who are venturing into this brave new world for the first time. Allow me to guide you through a few of the terms and basic Indian preparations. (You "old hands" might pick up a hint or two as well.)

Overall Note

Sometimes a recipe will call for an ingredient that will be chopped in a food processor along with other ingredients. Though not yet chopped, you may be asked for two tablespoons of, say, chilis. You'll need to eyeball a piece of that chili, or the number of chilis, that you think will end up being that amount were you to have chopped it separately.

Coconut Milk

The fast and easy out is canned or powdered. Canned coconut milk is available in almost all general food stores. Good, perhaps, but for the sake of the many food elite who would scoff at the notion of canned coconut milk in their curries, here are the two best methods to get at those raspy little rascals:

Your Own Coconut Milk Extracted from Brown Coconuts

The brown outer shell of the coconut is discarded. (In fact, the hairy outer husk, called "coir," is used to make rope.) The brown coating/skin on the surface of the coconut kernel may be ground with the coconut meat though some claim that it changes the color of the milk and they peel it off. Peeling it or not makes no difference to the curries appearing in this book.

After removing the hard external shell, the flesh is cut into manageable pieces and ground in a food processor with a bit of water to facilitate the process.

The thick mixture that results is squeezed through a single layer of cheese cloth. This first extraction is known as thick coconut milk. The coconut flesh can then be returned to the food processor to be ground again with more

water. The resultant liquid when squeezed through a cheese cloth is thin coconut milk.

Fresh coconut milk tends to curdle when it is boiled for a long period of time
or when it is put into an acidic medium so the cooking process begins with
thin coconut milk and is finished off and thickened with the first extraction,
the thick coconut milk.

Frankly, authenticity apart, and with a deferent bow to the "slow food move-
ment," I recommend cracking open a can of coconut milk (but not with your
mortar and pestle). Canned coconut milk of Thai origin, Maggi coconut milk
powder [I've never seen this in the U.S., ed.], and commercially available UHT
(ultra heat treated) coconut milk are great substitutes for the coconut extraction process. If you use any of these products, there is no need to concern yourself about first/second extract or thin/thick coconut milk. Just use the product
directly as there is little chance of these products curdling.

Coconut Milk from Desiccated Coconut

In areas where fresh coconut is not readily available, desiccated coconut may
be used. The method is similar. Place the desiccated coconut in a bowl and
cover with hot water. Allow it to reconstitute for ten to fifteen minutes and
then process in a food processor. Squeeze the milk out through cheese cloth,
following the instructions for fresh coconut above.

Tamarind

Tamarind is available in many forms though the treatment to achieve the use
of the pulp remains similar.

Tamarind cakes are a deseeded and compressed version of the fruit. During
manufacturing the fruit is processed whole, the seeds are removed, and it is
then simply pressed together.

Dried tamarind is the fresh fruit that has been sun-dried.

All one does is place the tamarind—fresh, cakes, or dried—into a pot, cover
with water and simmer for about twenty minutes. You will see a thick pulp
begin to form. Remove from the heat and set it aside to cool. Pass the pulp
through a sieve, discarding the fibrous remnants and use the sieved pulp as
needed. It can be stored refrigerated, in an air-tight jar, for something on the
order of a couple of months.

Panch-Phoran—How To Make It

This is a term used for a mixture of five spices, used predominantly in the cooking of the states of Bengal, Bihar and Orissa. This mixture is often referred to as Indian five-spice and is usually prepared in quantity at home and stored for later use.

A very simple method, making it involves mixing together equal quantities of fenugreek seeds, cumin seeds, fennel seeds, mustard seeds and onion seeds. When used, a pinch of the mixture is thrown into hot oil. When the spices crackle and release their aroma, the remainder of the dish's ingredients are added as per the recipe being followed.

Panch Phoran gives a finished dish a complex mélange of flavors. However, this mix does not lend itself easily to experimentation. It is best used within the confines of prescribed recipes.

How to Chop Onions
Without Adding the Salt of One's Tears

Legend has it that a delegation of onions went to petition Lord Brahma, the Hindu god of creation. They stated that they do gladly sacrifice their lives to enhance the palatability of humankind's meals yet they receive no thanks nor even brief mention. Invoking his divine powers and grace, Lord Brahma granted them great favor by proclaiming that whosoever shall cut onions from that day on would weep with pain in the memory of their slain brethren.

A touching story! However, it has done absolutely nothing to slack the tide of self-proclaimed experts who dish out their secret recipes to combat this effect. In my many years as a chef, I have witnessed numerous "cures" that range from the possibly believable to the flat-out bizarre.

Many believe in the power of a slice of bread held between one's teeth while chopping the onions. I was once even offered the suggestion that the bread should be buttered!

Indian kitchens call for great amounts of chopped onions to be used as a base for any of several curries, as a thickener, or as a filler. Onions, tasting wonderful when cooked, and being one of the cheapest vegetables at the market, they quickly gained a place of great use in many recipes—because they add flavor and deliver satiety at an economical price.

Indians prefer using sharp red onions to their milder flavored white cousins because they have less moisture and caramelize faster and because, in India, they are cheaper. In the U.S., red onions are commonly called Spanish onions, and the reverse is true; white onions caramelize more readily than red, and they are often cheaper.

What to do? You are faced with a basket full of onions requiring peeling and chopping. The easiest way to prevent crying yourself is to delegate the job to someone else. If your position in the home hierarchy grants no such privilege make sure that you are in a well ventilated area.

Always use a sharp knife to peel and cut. Onion cells contain a sulphur-based acid that is released into the air when cells are ruptured or broken. A sharp knife will cut more cleanly through the cell and allow less release of the juices containing the irritant to squirt all about. Placing the onions in a bowl of water after peeling them and quickly trashing the peels also tends to help a bit.

And now for something completely different. If my plan fails you are welcome to try a method that my pal Vishal swears by. He claims to have never cried while slicing onions because he keeps an onion circle tucked on his left ear. He hasn't yet figured out how to get his wife, Saloni, to ignore the smell that lingers into the evening!

How To Cook Onions

Onions have been around for more than five thousand years. Ancient Vedic texts mention them, as do Sumerian writings, ancient Egyptian scrolls, and there is a brief mention in the Biblical book of Numbers.

Onions were originally believed to have mystical properties. The great Indian physician Charaka (c. 300 B.C.E.) mentions their antiseptic properties as well as their diuretic capabilities. The ancient Egyptians invested this humble vegetable with revered mystical qualities, interpreting its circle within a circle structure to represent infinity. They used onion in their mummification process in the hope that the dead would find them useful in the afterlife.

Some societies in ancient India banned the consumption of onions or garlic to widows, celibates, and sages because the carnal lust onions promote would cause the loss of status or concentration during meditation.

Onions were used in the treatment of cholera and thought to slake the patient's thirst.

Given that basic trivia about onions, what do they really do? They can be pickled rather easily They can be dried so they keep for long periods of time. But, most importantly, they are vital to Indian cookery.

In India, onions are among the cheapest vegetables one can obtain. Since economics is often a prime factor in the consideration of diet and many vegetables prove expensive to a significant portion of the population, large quantities of onions were used to bulk up meals. When cooked, onions are a great thickener and they impart a characteristic sweetness that helps to balance other tastes in the dish.

Indians take the browning of their onions seriously. Traditionally a lot of oil is used to ensure that the onions are well browned which in turn results in the final product having a distinct oily feel to it, but the rich flavor of the carmelization caused by frying them brown is what's important.

When onions are immersed in oil at high heat, moisture from the onions evaporates rapidly and the onions brown faster and more evenly. Some Indians deep fry sliced onions until they are golden and crisp before grinding them.

Most dishes call for onions to be cooked until they are golden brown. Care must be taken because there is a fine line dividing desirable golden brown from acrid "golden" black. Simmering the onions while occasionally stirring them is the best way to ensure that they are cooked to perfection. I prefer a copper pot or a non-stick casserole. Stainless steel heats faster and causes the onions to stick and burn if they are not carefully watched. A convenient but not so healthy option (if you have a deep cooker always at the ready) has some chefs separately deep fry the onions until they are golden, processing them to a paste. They use this in curries to eliminate their diners coming across partially cooked onions—which among Indians is equivalent to culinary heresy.

How to Make Ginger Paste

Grind peeled ginger in a food processor with an amount of water that will result in a paste. Indian provisioners carry pre-packaged ginger paste or you can use finely chopped ginger as a substitute.

How to Store Fresh Herbs

Coriander leaves, fresh mint and dill leaves are three herbs often used in Indian cuisine. Storing them so they retain their vitality is of great importance, especially in areas where they are not easy to obtain fresh.

The best method I have come across is to cut off the roots, place the herbs stem first into a bowl of steaming hot water so that they are immersed halfway up their shoots and then place the entire lot into a refrigerator. Herbs tend to stay fresh for about ten days this way. Whenever you find your herbs drooping, discard the old water and repeat the process.

While that is the best method, if you don't have enough space in your refrigerator, wash the herbs well, flick them hard in the air to release the water trapped between the leaves, roll them in two sheets of kitchen paper toweling, enclose them in a plastic bag and refrigerate. In this manner they should stay fresh for about a week.

Another method for keeping some greens longer is similar. Do not rinse. Leave the roots on when they are present and wrap the bottoms of the stalks of leafy greens only high enough to get a grasp, in a sheet of wetted (but not dripping) paper toweling. Put them in a plastic bag with a twist tie at the top, evacuating as much air as possible by compressing, or use a plastic straw stuck through the turns of the plastic bag before it is tied, to suck out as much air as possible. I've had coriander keep this way for nearly a month.

The Cooking of Spices

Indians use both whole and ground spices in their food preparation. The whole spices used most usually are cumin, cinnamon, cardamom, and cloves; the ground spices used most usually are chili, turmeric and coriander powders.

Many recipes begin with the rapid and brief heating of whole spices in hot oil or ghee while ground spices are brought into the recipe at a later stage as they have a tendency to stick to the bottom and burn.

Adding whole spices to hot fat cause them to swell, crackle, and turn golden, releasing their flavor to the oil and their aroma to the air. This is the ideal time to immediately begin the next stage of the recipe. If the spices are allowed to heat for longer, they will burn and spread a bitter taste to the entire dish.

To avoid concentrating powdered spices, thus allowing them to be more easily incorporated into thick sauces in preparation, mix powdered spices with a bit of water to form a paste, only then adding it to the pot.

Roasting spices before pounding them to a powder helps to enhance their fragrance and aroma. Add the spices individually to a hot, heavy, dry pan until they begin to change color. Then grind them to a powder or pulverize them using a mortar and pestle.

Much as the French technique for preparing a roux requires slow, steady heat, when powdered spices are added one must continually stir them at a simmer for five minutes or more. This enables the raw flavor of the spice to cook out. Should one fail to do this, the finished dish will have overtones of the raw spice.

The Art of Tempering

Unlike the rapid heating of whole spices, tempering is the traditional Indian process of simmering oil or ghee with spices to impart their flavor to the oil. This flavored oil is then added to the finished dish just prior to serving, thus enhancing the flavors and adding complexity.

You may continue the practice of budding chefs, who have over several centuries experimented with the spices and the amounts used in tempering the oil, thereby occasionally introducing to the cuisine over time, astounding new results.

Ancient medical treatises document the work of physicians who prescribed spice-infused oils for their therapeutic value as massage mediums to relieve pain. In a natural progression people began to ingest these oils in order to obtain their maximum result. It was not a great leap to impart this wonderful mélange and complexity of flavor to spice up a dish thus gaining immediate culinary recognition and acceptance.

The spice mixture used in the tempering process is a clear indication of the region of India from which a dish hails. The spices and other ingredients that are added will vary somewhat depending on the season or the experimental nature of the person preparing the meal. It's likely, for example, that a recipe from the southern states will include at least a few grains of lentils in the tempering. This imparts a nuttiness to the result

Regardless of the known health hazards, most Indians love to see a gleaming layer of oil spread across the stuff we intend to eat. One doesn't really need much oil to impart flavor and zing to a dish. The north seems to prefer ghee, the central and eastern regions like mustard oil, and the southern areas lean toward coconut oil. The basic methods of tempering, however, remain the same. A rule-of-thumb recipe for basic tempering follows.

For each 400 g/2 cups of a finished dish such as lentils and sauces you will need:

Oil or ghee (I prefer ghee most of the time)	30 g/1½ tbsp
Cumin seeds	3 g/½ tsp
Fresh chilies, chopped	10 g

Heat the oil and add the cumin seeds. When they crackle, add the fresh chilies and simmer for a few minutes. Pour this mixture over the dish to be tempered and stir it in to blend the flavors.

How to Sprout Beans

Moong/Mung sprouts are quite easy to prepare. While there is expensive equipment available to aid this process there are alternative methods that require only basic kitchen inventory.

Immerse the whole moong beans in warm water and leave them to soak for five hours or so. Spread and moisten paper kitchen towels on a work surface. Drain and spread the soaked beans on the paper, covering them with more sheets of kitchen paper towels or cloth kitchen towels. Sprinkle a bit of water over the top towels so as to lightly moisten them. Leave the beans in a cool place for fifteen to eighteen hours to sprout. Use them as needed.

Steaming:

In India we have several varieties of commercially available steaming devices that are quite similar in function to a vegetable steamer or Chinese dim sum steamer. Most homes that do not have a commercial steamer will improvise from items available. As the requirements are really simple, there are a variety of ways one can create one's own steamer.

The easiest method is the pot method. A pot is filled with water to a depth sufficient that it will not boil away. An overturned bowl is placed in the pot as a makeshift platform and water reaching part way up the bowl is brought to a boil. The molds or tray are placed on the bowl such that they are well above the water level. The pot is covered with a well-fitting lid and steam is allowed to build within the pot, thus steaming the food.

The other method involves the use of a pressure cooker. Place the trays or molds in a similar fashion in a pressure cooker with a satisfactory level of boiling water and seal the lid, but leave the whistle off, thereby allowing the steam to escape, or otherwise prevent pressure from building in the pot.

How Well Do You Know Your Curry?

Like all things Indian, diversity has made its way into our cuisine. When my mother cooks, she can make the same curry in a hundred different ways. (It helps that she regularly forgets the correct ingredients and their sequence.)

Regional indicators play a large role in discovering where your curry originated. Styles of food are influenced by the produce regionally available, history, religious practices in the region, and the economic factors that govern the majority of the populace.

When we refer to the northern states in India, we speak of Kashmir, Punjab, Delhi, Uttar Pradesh (creators of the famous Awadhi cuisine based on slow cooking; see http://en.wikipedia.org/wiki/Awadhi_cuisine) and parts of Madhya Pradesh, Rajasthan and Bihar. One finds a lot of star anise used in Kashmir, cinnamon in Himachal Pradesh, and other whole spices used in Punjab and Delhi. The food in the north is rich, teems with ghee, and, often, cream and butter. The use of wheat, tandoor-style cooking (Indian clay oven), and whole spices are distinguishing characteristics.

There is an element of Muslim influence that is seen in the kebabs and biryanis. Curries are flavored with a variety of whole spices. Saffron is often used, with onion and tomatoes employed as a method to thicken their curries.

Bihar, Bengal and Orissa that lie toward the east use mustard oil in their food. These regions also regularly use Panch Phoran, the spice mix discussed on page 36.

Rajasthan and Gujarat often use yogurt as the base for their curries with a dash of asafoetida to compensate in flavor for the lack of onions and garlic in their food. There is a tendency to use dried red chilies as the region is a leading producer of these chilis; each variety of chili seeking to rival another in terms of its heat. Here curries may be thickened by the addition of gram flour.

Food from Goa shows a historic influence from Portugal and their colonies in Africa. The use of vinegar as a souring agent, much coconut milk, and the use of chili pastes is a giveaway in pinpointing Goa's traditional curries.

Curries from the southern states may be thickened with lentils or coconut milk. Its food is flavored largely with mustard seeds, dried red chilies, curry leaves, and a pinch of roasted lentils that imparts a nutty flavor to the food.

Not surprisingly, as beaches are where much coconut is found, the coastal regions use a lot of coconut in their curries. This may be in the form of coconut oil, grated coconut, or coconut milk, or all of them together.

In the present era of globalization, many influences have travelled about, fusing themselves as inextricable parts of a cuisine, so these broad indicators are just that--broad indicators that soon may just designate historic origins.

Basic Curries and Sauces

Basic sauces can be made ahead and kept refrigerated from five days to a week. A significant change in quality is not observed even if they have been frozen for a month, defrosted, and then used. I suggest the use of portion-sized containers for storage to avoid defrosting the entire batch when all you require is enough to prepare a meal for two. You may freeze the sauce in ice-cube trays. Store the frozen sauce cubes in plastic freezer bags.

After refrigeration or freezing, sauce becomes of uneven texture. This tends to make reheating difficult unless one adds a bit of water to smooth it out again. Begin by adding ¼ cup (50 ml) of water, gradually increasing the amount, as necessary, during the heating process. The added moisture prevents the sauce from burning and sticking to the bottom of the pot. Stir constantly, bringing the gravy to the consistency you prefer. This can depend on whether you intend to ladle it over precooked food or use it as a thinner cooking base in which foods will simmer.

Always simmer sauce on low to medium heat and stir it frequently. Indian spices have a tendency to accumulate at the bottom of the pot and burn. The burned flavor will permeate the sauce, ruining it.

When using a premade sauce as the stock in which vegetables are to be cooked, there are a few adjustments that need to be made when using a general recipe. Potatoes, sweet potatoes and almost all varieties of tubers tend to absorb a lot of water during cooking, while okra, string beans, baby corn, mushrooms and leafy greens do not. This should be taken into consideration in adding water to the sauce prior to cooking. More can be added as the process goes along and one sees the sauce thickening too much.

Experimentation has been the base of the Indian culinary tradition over the centuries and you should feel free to mix and match sauces to suit your tastes. The only care one should take is to ensure that the sauces are stored individually and mixed together only in the pot in which the curry is to be cooked. The standards, those most-used Indian sauces have self-adjusted over the centuries to have a compatibility with each other that enables widely different-tasting sauces to blend together on the plate into yet another and ever-varying taste sensation as the meal is eaten. This ability seems to exist equally well in no other cuisine.

When adding green vegetables like string beans, peas, okra or snow peas to a curry sauce, do so toward the end of the cooking process. The vegetables will remain a bright green and will not become overcooked.

Basic Curry Sauce

This recipe results in a delicious, no-frills curry leaving you free to choose the ingredients you will cook in it.

A useful feature of this recipe is that the sauce can be made well in advance. It will keep in the refrigerator for a week to ten days and almost indefinitely in the freezer. You can double or even quadruple this recipe, reserving the result to be used as needed. Whenever you like, pull out a bit of this sauce, cook up your choice of vegetables, and presto! you'll have what is literally "A curry in a hurry."

Oil	30 ml/⅛ cup
Cumin seeds	a pinch
Cinnamon stick	1 piece, about 2–3 inches in length
Green cardamom	4 pods
Onions, chopped	150g/¾ cup
Tomatoes, chopped	100g/½ cup
Red chili powder	10g/½ tbsp (or to preferred heat)
Turmeric	10g/½ tbsp
Salt	10g/½ tbsp

Heat the oil in a heavy-bottomed pot. Add the cumin, cinnamon and cardamom. When the spices begin to swell and change color, add the onions and stir until they are golden. Add the tomatoes and simmer until they turn pulpy. Add the chili powder, turmeric, and salt and continue to stir on low heat for about five minutes. Remove from heat.

Create a basic curry sauce concentrate by adding 2 cups (400 ml) of water, bring it to a boil for a minute and simmer for ten minutes to incorporate the spices.

When ready to prepare a dish, introduce as much sauce as you think the vegetables need in order to cook. Simmer them in the sauce until the vegetables reach your preferred state of doneness. If they are vegetables that tend to take up water (potatoes, parsnip) you will want to add some water before starting them to cook. If your choice of vegetables tend to give up water (onion, celery, mushrooms) or you have added too much water to begin with, you may want to reduce the volume of liquid by removing the vegetables when they are done and simmer until the sauce reaches the consistency you'd like

Tip: Common usage of the word "gravy" dictates that gravy will contain or have been made from meat. "Sauce," on the other hand, contains no meat. In the Anglicized Indian context, we tend to call most of our curries "gravies" even if they are vegetarian. Therefore, you will find gravy and sauce used interchangeably throughout this book.

Basic Korma

A korma is a cream- and nut-enriched gravy that came to fame in the royal banquet halls of the Mughal emperors. The center of power of the ancient Mughal Empire was in Delhi, which is in that part of the subcontinent that sees the most severe winters. Hardly considered even "bracing" by a crusty New Englander, the temperature can get below 50°F in January or February. In such adverse conditions a korma is considered a good "warmer," generating enough heat within the body to ward off the winter chills.

Cashew nuts	30 g/6 tsp
Oil or Ghee	20 g/1 tbsp
Cinnamon stick	1 piece, about 2–3 inches in length
Green cardamom	4 pods
Cloves	4 buds
Onions, chopped	50 g/¼ cup
Garlic, chopped	10 g/2 tsp
Ginger, shredded	10 g/2 tsp
Tomatoes, chopped	40 g/2 tbsp
Turmeric	5 g/1 tsp
Fresh chilis, chopped	5 g/1 tsp
Salt	5 g/1 tsp
Cream	50 ml/¼ cup

Soak the cashew nuts in warm water for about fifteen minutes. Remove from water and grind them to a smooth paste in a food processor. Reserve for later use.

Heat the oil or ghee in a heavy-bottomed pot and add the cinnamon, cardamom and cloves. When the spices begin to swell and change color, add the onions and cook them on gentle heat until they are golden. Add the garlic and ginger and stir until they soften Add the tomatoes, turmeric, green chilis, and salt and simmer until the tomatoes are pulpy. Stir in the cashew nut paste, simmer for a minute, and add ½ cup (100 ml) of water and the cream. Simmer until the gravy boils and begins to thicken. Remove from heat.

This korma will keep refrigerated for about five days. When you wish to use the sauce, reheat it and add the ingredients that you intend to cook along with an appropriate quantity of water to cook the vegetables. Simmer until they are done.

Basic Masala (Gravy)

A masala is a thickened sauce that is meant to coat the ingredients added to it. (The word is also used to describe a mixture of dry spices.) It is a little spicier and noticeably thicker than a curry. A general practice in the northern parts of India is to enrich gravies by adding large quantities of ghee or oil. This should not be done. The effect of this purported "improved" taste is overcome by the oily sensation it has while eating it.

Oil	40 ml/2 tbsp
Cinnamon stick	1 piece, about 2–3 inches in length
Green cardamom	3 pods
Cloves	4 buds
Onions, chopped	200 g/1 cup
Garlic, chopped	20 g/1 tbsp
Ginger, chopped	10 g/2 tsp
Fresh chilis, chopped	20 g/1 tbsp
Tomato, chopped	150 g/¾ cup
Turmeric	10 g/2 tsp
Coriander seeds, roasted	5 g/1 tsp
Coriander leaves, chopped	5 g/1 tsp

Heat the oil in a heavy-bottomed pan. Add the cinnamon, cardamom and cloves. When the spices begin to swell and change color, add the onions and cook until they are golden. Add the garlic and ginger and simmer until the garlic turns soft. Add the chilis, tomatoes, and turmeric and stir on high heat until the tomatoes begin to soften. Gently crush the coriander seeds in your palm with your fingers and sprinkle over the mixture. Stir in the coriander leaves and remove from the heat. Let cool

This sauce will keep refrigerated for about a week.

Masalas

Garam Masala

The most well known of Indian spice mixes, garam masala can be easily bought, even in supermarkets, but freshly ground and mixed garam masala has its own different and delightful fragrance and flavor. It is best prepared fresh every day. If that is not possible, then make a batch and store it in an airtight container and keep it in a cool place to minimize its loss of fragrance. (For a discussion on how to roast spices, see page 39)

Black peppercorns	20 g/1 tbsp
Cumin seeds	20 g/1 tbsp
Cloves	25 buds
Bay leaves	5
Mace	3 g/½ tsp
Cinnamon sticks	2 pieces, about 2–3 inches in length
Nutmeg, freshly grated	1
Black cardamom	3 pods
Green cardamom	6 pods

Roast the spices individually until they are golden. Pound them in a mortar with a pestle or grind them together to a fine powder in a spice grinder or small food processor. Store the garam masala in an airtight jar until it is needed. It is used during cooking, or to finish off a dish.

Chaat Masala

Although commercial packets of this spice mix are available at many Indian provision stores, a spice mixture always benefits from fresh preparation. You may simply enjoy preparing your own version. This savory spice mix is used to sprinkle onto many chaat preparations.

Cumin seeds/jeera, roasted	10 g/2 tsp
Black peppercorns, roasted	5 g/1 tsp
Ginger, powdered	5 g/1 tsp
Black rock salt/kala namak, crushed	20 g/1 tbsp
Green mango powder/Amchoor	25 g/5 tsp
Salt	5 g/1 tsp

Grind the ingredients together in a spice grinder or small food processor until they become a coarse powder. Store in an airtight jar until needed.

Rasam Powder

Rasam Podi

This is the basic spice mix required for a rasam (soup). In the south of India, where rasams are usually prepared daily, it is not uncommon to make this spice mix in large quantities to be stored in airtight containers for later use.

Red chilis, dried	150 g/¾ cup
Coriander seeds	75 g/⅜ cup
Cumin seeds	20 g/1 tbsp
Fenugreek /Methi seeds	10 g/2 tsp
Mustard Seeds	15 g/3 tsp

In a dry pan, dry roast the ingredients separately. Stir or toss them frequently to prevent burning. Cool and grind them to a fine powder. Store in an airtight container for later use.

Vegetable Masala Powder

This spice mixture can be used as a flavoring sprinkle for vegetable dishes and pulao (pilaf).

Dried red chilis	100 g/½ cup
Coriander seeds	50 g/¼ cup
Cumin seeds	5 g/1 tsp

Mustard seeds	5 g/1 tsp
Bengal gram	10 g/2 tsp
Moong dal	10 g/2 tsp
Rice, uncooked	10 g/2 tsp
Ginger, chopped	10 g/2 tsp
Fenugreek seeds	5 g/1 tsp
Whole turmeric	5 g/1 tsp

(use powdered turmeric if whole is unavailable)

Dry roast all the ingredients and grind them to a fine powder in a spice grinder or small food processor; mix and keep in an airtight jar for later use.

Do Indians Eat Soup?

Soup came to the subcontinent with the Europeans. Shorbas, yakhnis and rasams are the closest Indians come to having soup represent a significant part of a meal. The idea of having soup as a separate course is almost unknown in Indian cuisine.

Soups are thought of by Indians as a way to stimulate hunger and as an aid to digestion. A spicy, fragrant, tangy soup helps stimulate appetite which enables consuming a greater quantity of more solid foods. So, if you're one of those Westerners who thinks that "Is it soup yet?" is a call to a complete meal, think again. While your soup will be vibrant and tasty, be prepared for it to seem somewhat "thin."

Soups in India are served with the main part of the meal. Indians have never quite understood the Western concept of filling the stomach with a liquid as a separate course. It is thought better to drink it during the meal as one would occasionally sip water. It is definitely a tastier alternative.

Yakhnis, brought to India by the invading Mughal armies, are what one would think of as a garnished, flavorful stock. They are meat-based and result from long simmering. Shorbas, often vegetable-based, originated in the north where they were developed to enable vegetarian courtiers to partake of soup, while rasams, which are quite similar, developed simultaneously in the south.

Called shorbas in the north, and rasams in the south, Indian soups do not generally use a stock base as they are served with all the ingredients that they are prepared with, relying on the spices and herbs put in them to impart the desired flavor. Unlike many other cuisines, most Indian soups use only water as the cooking liquid. The flavorings and ingredients of the soup are neither strained nor processed further thereby providing the flavor and retaining the unique taste of its constituents.

More than four hundred years of British rule has not overwhelmed the cuisine of India. However, it did force several generations of servers and chefs attached to European or European-influenced households to rethink the notions they held about soups. The result is the addition of a list of absolutely delicious soups to India's already rich, deep, and mature culinary repertoire.

In India, most soups are made quite thin as their purpose is more to whet the appetite than to satisfy it. Being passionate about the food on their plate, they hate to think of a wimpy soup as denying them any portion of their fill of calorie-laden and satisfying main entrees and desserts.

Spinach and Coconut Milk Soup
Palak aur Nariyal ka Shorba

During a visit to the local quack, the parents of Rajan, a friend in my youth, were advised that Rajan was to be fed a diet rich in spinach. This did not seem at first a terrible ordeal, but his parents soon let their fears drag them from reality. Each dish in every meal had spinach lurking about somewhere. When Rajan revolted, his parents cajoled me into joining him for mealtimes in order that I would help them forward their program. Well, in actuality, Rajan's mom made an excellent go of it. This soup has stood out in my memory since then.

Spinach leaves, thoroughly rinsed	400 g/2 cups
Oil	20 ml/1 tbsp
Garlic, chopped	10 g/2 tsp
Fennel seeds	5 g/1 tsp
Ginger, shredded	5 g/1 tsp
Coconut milk	600 ml/3 cups
Salt	to taste

Boil the spinach leaves in the merest amount of salted water, or add no water, using just the water that's left after rinsing the leaves. When they have turned a bright green, allow them to cool, drain, and process them to a thin paste in a food processor.

Heat the oil in a heavy-bottomed pan and add the chopped garlic and fennel seeds. Stir on low heat until they change color. Add the pureed spinach and stir for a few minutes. Add two cups (400 ml) of water, the ginger, coconut milk and salt. Simmer for twenty minutes until the soup has thickened sufficiently. Taste and adjust the seasoning if necessary. Serve hot.

Tips: Coconut milk reduces in volume and thickens during prolonged cooking. Boil this soup for a longer time to get a thicker soup, if that's what you want.

Canned coconut milk from Thailand is best and readily available.

Carrot and Carom Seed Soup
Ajwaini Gajar ka Shorba

Oil	20 ml/1 tbsp
Carom seeds/ajwain	a pinch
Carrots, peeled and diced	400 g/2 cups
Onions, chopped	30 g/2 tbsp
Garlic, chopped	10 g/2 tsp
Ginger, shredded	5 g/1 tsp
Black peppercorns, crushed	5 g/1 tsp
Salt	to taste
Coriander leaves, chopped	5 g/1 tsp

Heat the oil in a heavy-bottomed pan and add the carom seeds. When they splutter, add the carrots, onions, and garlic. Stir on low heat for about ten minutes until the carrots soften somewhat and the onions are transparent. Remove from heat, cool, and process to a smooth puree in a food processor.

Return the puree to the pan along with 2 cups (400 ml) of water, ginger, peppercorns and salt. Simmer for about fifteen minutes until the soup is suitably thickened. Taste and adjust seasoning if necessary. Finish with the coriander leaves and serve hot.

Tip: Carom seeds are bitter if used in excess, so restrict a pinch to just that.

Lentil Soup
Dal ka Shorba

Red lentils/Masoor dal	50 g/¼ cup
Oil	10 ml/2 tsp
Cumin seeds	a pinch
Fresh chili, slit (see page 29)	1
Turmeric powder–	a pinch
Salt	to taste
Coriander leaves, chopped	3 g/½ tsp
Lemon wedges	2

Wash the lentils in ample running water; soak for twenty minutes; drain the excess water.

In a heavy-bottomed pan, heat the oil and add the cumin seeds. When the seeds crackle, add the lentils and stir them in the pan until they are opaque, add the turmeric, the salt and the slit green chili. Stir for two more minutes and then add 1 ½ cups (300 ml) of water.

Reduce the heat and simmer the lentils about 10 minutes or until they are soft and shapeless. Taste and adjust the seasoning if required. Finish with the chopped coriander leaves and serve hot with a lemon wedge.

Tip: Soaking the lentils in water for twenty minutes before cooking will reduce the cooking time to half.

Tomato Soup
Tamatar ka Shorba

Tomatoes, chopped	200g/1 cup
Carrots, peeled and thinly sliced	50 g/¼ cup
Green cardamom	3 pods
Ginger, peeled	5 g/1 tsp
Fresh chili, slit (see page 29)	1
Salt	to taste
Sugar	5 g/1 tsp
Coriander leaves, chopped-	5 g/1 tsp

Chop the tomatoes roughly and place them in a heavy-bottomed pot along with the carrots, cardamom, ginger, green chili, salt, and sugar. Add a quart (liter) of water and simmer for half an hour until the carrots are soft. Increase the heat to bring the contents to a boil and skim off any scum that may rise to the surface.

Press the contents of the pot through a strainer using a round-bottomed spoon or other implement to ensure minimum wastage.

Discard the vegetables that remain in the strainer.

Adjust the flavor and consistency if necessary. Bring to a boil, finish with the fresh coriander leaves, and serve hot.

Tip: This is a thin soup. For a thicker soup, blend all the ingredients in a food processor until they are smooth and then strain the result.

Tomato-Pineapple Rasam

Rasams are spicy soups that originated in the southern parts of India.

Toovar dal/yellow lentils, washed and drained	75 g/⅜cup
Ginger, shredded	5 g/1 tsp
Turmeric–	a pinch
Crush and roast together, a pinch each of coriander seeds, cumin seeds, fenugreek seeds.	
Oil	20 ml/1 tbsp
Mustard seeds (roasted separately)	a pinch
Red chilis, dried	3
Curry leaves	one sprig
Pineapple, chopped	50 g/¼ cup
Tomatoes, finely chopped	40 g/2 tbsp
Garlic, chopped	5 g/1 tsp
Pineapple juice	40 ml/2 tbsp
Tamarind pulp extract	10 ml/½ tbsp
Salt	to taste

In a pot, place the lentils, ginger, turmeric, and two cups (400 ml) of water. Bring to a boil. Skim off the scum that rises to the surface. Add the crushed coriander, cumin, and fennel seeds, simmering all until the lentils are soft but not mushy. Remove from heat.

In a separate heavy-bottomed pan, heat the oil and add the mustard seeds. When they splutter, stir in the chilis and the curry leaves. When the leaves crackle, reduce the heat, and add the garlic to cook slowly until it is golden. Blend in the tomatoes and pineapple and simmer until the tomatoes are soft. Add the pineapple juice, the tamarind pulp, and the lentils with their cooking liquid, and salt, to taste. Simmer for five more minutes, taste and adjust seasoning if necessary. Serve hot.

Tips: This is a very watery soup. You can increase the lentils to add body.

If the soup lies undisturbed for even brief periods, the lentils tend to sink to the bottom leaving the spiced, watery part at the surface. Stir a couple of times while ladling out the soup.

Pumpkin Soup

Kadoo ka Champoo

Raju, a friend, and the present not-so-good guardian of what was once an old secret family recipe, recounted to me the story of how this dish got its strange name (the Indian name, Kadoo ka Champoo).

It is said that one of Raju's ancestors was a chief cook attached to a princely family who once prepared this soup for his masters and their guest, the British commanding officer of the local garrison.

Part way through the meal, the cook was commanded to appear in the dining hall before his masters. Fearing the worst, and trembling at his fate, the man approached the great hall with increasingly heavy footsteps. His master, far from being upset, was greatly pleased because his honored guest had expressed extreme happiness and satisfaction with the soup. When asked its name, the now highly stressed cook came out with the first few words that he could muster. Thus, here follows the recipe for a soup that translates from slang to mean a shaved pumpkin.

Pumpkin, peeled and cut into cubes	400 g/2 cups
Potatoes, peeled and diced	200 g/1 cup
Onions, sliced	50 g/¼ cup
Garlic, peeled	10 g/2 tsp
Ginger, peeled	10 g/2 tsp
Black peppercorns	6
Turmeric	3 g/½ tsp
Salt	to taste
Oil	20 ml/1 tbsp
Asafoetida/hing	a pinch
Mustard seeds	a pinch
Cumin seeds	a pinch
Dried chilis, cut in half	2
Mint leaves, shredded	5 g/1 tsp
Juice of one lemon	

Fill a pot with two quarts/two liters of water and boil together the pumpkin, potatoes, onions, garlic, ginger, peppercorns, turmeric and salt. When the vegetables are tender, about twenty minutes, retain the cooking liquid, but strain out the vegetables and process them to a smooth puree in a food processor. Return the puree to the pot with the retained liquid. Simmer for ten minutes or more, until the soup has thickened sufficiently that it coats the back of a spoon.

Heat the oil in a heavy-bottomed pan and add the asafoetida, mustard, cumin, and chilis. When the seeds crackle, pour this mixture into the soup and incorporate well. Add the mint leaves, the lemon juice, and stir a few times. Remove to a serving bowl, taste, and adjust the seasoning, if required. Serve hot.

Tip: Hard-skinned pumpkin can be very difficult and potentially dangerous to peel. Use a sharp peeler and lay the pumpkin flat on your work surface. Peel away from your body

Tip: This soup works equally well with roasted pumpkin, avoiding the need to remove the outer skin. Cut the pumpkin into large pieces and put them in a preheated oven (180*C/375*F) for twenty minutes until the pulp is soft. Scrape off and discard the seeds. Scoop out the softened pulp and add it to the soup after the potatoes have softened.

Onion-Pepper Soup

Kaandhechya Rassa

In Maharashra, a state that often sees a bumper crop of onions as well as a really hot summer, the residents have created from their very available ingredients a very refreshing soup. This spicy soup will cause perspiration, afterward leaving the skin feeling cooler.

Onions, chopped	400 g/2 cups
Oil	20 ml/1 tbsp
Cumin seeds	3 g/½ tsp
Lightly crushed coriander seeds	3 g/½ tsp
Fresh chilis, slit (see page 29)	2
Tomatoes, chopped	40 g/2 tbsp
Tamarind pulp	10 g/½ tbsp
Ginger, shredded	10 g/2 tsp

Black peppercorns, crushed	20 g/1 tbsp
Sugar	a pinch
Salt	to taste
Coriander leaves, chopped	5 g/1 tsp

Heat the oil in a heavy-bottomed pan. Add the cumin and coriander seeds. When they crackle, add the onions and gently simmer until they are golden. Add the green chilis, tomatoes and a quart/liter of water and simmer for twenty minutes. Add the tamarind pulp, ginger, peppercorns, sugar and salt and simmer until the tomatoes turn pulpy. Taste and adjust the seasoning if required. Remove from the heat, stir in the coriander leaves, and serve hot.

You can give this traditional soup an additional twist by adding in some asparagus tips or sliced mushrooms toward the end of the cooking time.

Beetroot and Fennel Soup

Chukandar ka Rassa

Beetroots, peeled and cut into 1-inch cubes	400 g/2 cups
Oil	40 ml/2 tbsp
Fennel seeds	a pinch
Green cardamom	5 pods
Chopped ginger	10 g/2 tsp
Fresh chilies, Chopped	10 g/2 tsp
Salt	to taste
Coconut milk	400 ml/2 cups
Black peppercorns, crushed	a pinch
Juice of one lemon	
Mint leaves, chopped	10 g/2 tsp

Heat the oil in a thick-bottomed pot adding the fennel seeds and cardamom. When the spices begin to change color, add the beetroot and stir for five minutes on medium heat.

Add ginger, fresh chilies, and salt, stirring for a few more minutes. Pour in 400 ml/2 cups of water. Bring to a rapid boil for a minute and then simmer for twenty minutes until the beetroot is soft. Blend the beets in a food processor and return the mix to the heat.

Add the coconut milk and simmer until the mixture thickens to coating consistency. Taste and adjust the seasonings, if necessary,

Remove from the heat, stir in the crushed black pepper, lemon juice, and mint leaves and serve hot.

Papads, Pakoras, and Plenty of Taste

Tangy Potato-and-Green-Pea-Stuffed Fried Papad

Papad rolls

Along with the British Raj, many European cultural practices and expectations moved into India. Parties that earlier would have focused on a lavish buffet now required much culinary innovation to satisfy the new penchant for hors d'oeuvres and finger-foods. Traditional Indian snacks were refined to have aesthetic appearance while retaining their original taste. Of the senses that appeal to a diner, taste and fragrance (to the near exclusion of the others) are favored by Indians. However, this recipe surpasses expectation and delights all the senses.

Papads (referred to often as papadum in the U.S.) are flat lentil wafers purchased ready made. They are available at many supermarkets and almost all Indian and Asian stores.

Potatoes, boiled, peeled and mashed	250 g/1¼ cups
Green peas	75 g/⅓ cup
Oil	20 ml/1 tbsp
Cumin seeds	5 g/1 tsp
Carom seeds/Ajwain	3 g/½ tsp
Fresh chilis, chopped	10 g/2 tsp
Ginger, shredded	5 g/1 tsp
Turmeric	5 g/1 tsp
Salt	to taste
Coriander leaves, chopped	5 g/1 tsp
Papads	12
Bengal gram flour/Besan	40 g/2 tbsp
Chaat masala (see page 49)	5 g/1 tsp
Oil	to deep fry papads

Heat 20 ml/1 tbsp oil in a heavy-bottomed pan and add the cumin and carom seeds. When the seeds crackle, add the potatoes, green peas, green chilis, turmeric, and salt. Toss the vegetables over low heat, stirring the entire time until the green peas are tender and done. Taste and adjust the seasoning, if required. Finish with the coriander leaves and reserve the stuffing for later use.

Leave the papads in the packet and fold the packet in half pressing along the folded edge. This will break the papads in half. Separately blend the gram flour with enough water to make a thick paste that will be used later as a glue.

Using a spray bottle, if available, lightly dampen the papad half with a bit of water to make it pliable. Place a bit of the potato-green pea stuffing at one side of the papad and roll it toward the other side so that the filling stays firmly inside it, much in the manner of an Italian *cannoli*. Secure the trailing edge in place with the gram flour paste.

Deep fry in a wok or kadhai in hot oil until it is golden and crisp. Drain the excess oil onto an absorbent kitchen paper towel or brown paper. Sprinkle with chaat masala and serve hot.

Vegetable Patties

Vegetable Chaap

Bengali "chaap" has grown to become an institution. What had begun as a vegetarian version of British Raj cuisine, has grown to dominate the menus at most canteens, cafeterias, stadiums and railway stations throughout India.

The appeal of this dish lies in its sheer simplicity of preparation. It can be eaten as a snack or gorged on to make it a complete meal.

Oil	20 ml/1 tbsp
Cumin seeds	5 g/1 tsp
Onions, chopped	40 g/2 tbsp
Carrots, grated	70 g/⅓ cup
Cauliflower, chopped	40 g/2 tbsp
Green peas	40 g/2 tbsp
Potatoes, boiled, peeled and mashed	100 g/½ cup
Turmeric	5 g/1 tsp
Chili powder	5 g/1 tsp
Coriander powder	5 g/1 tsp

Gram flour	20 g/1 tbsp
Coriander leaves, chopped	10 g/2 tsp
Spinach, rinsed and torn	50g/½ cup
Flour	20 g/1 tbsp
Bread crumbs	70 g/⅓ cup
Oil	to deep fry

Heat the oil in a heavy-bottomed pan and add the cumin seeds. When the seeds crackle, add the onions and sauté until they are golden. Add the carrots, cauliflower and green peas and cook for about five minutes on low heat, stirring occasionally. Add the potatoes, spinach, turmeric, chili, and coriander powders, salt, and gram flour and continue to stir and cook until the spices have melded and all the moisture has been evaporated. Stir in the coriander leaves. Taste and adjust the seasoning if necessary. Remove the mixture from the heat and put aside to cool.

Separately whisk together the flour with enough water to make a thin batter that just coats the mixing spoon.

Form the cooked vegetables into golf ball-sized balls. Dip them in the batter and roll them in the bread crumbs until they are evenly coated. Flatten the balls in the palm of your hands to form them into inch-thick discs. Fry them in medium-hot oil until they are crisp, a process that should take about five minutes. Serve hot with ketchup.

Ketchup? Ketchup? What can I say about the West corrupting the culinary innocence of my fellow Indians. Yes, Indians do consume a fair bit of Heinz (and local brands like Kissan and Noga). The use of ketchup is quite common in several parts of the country.

If the suggestion of ketchup appals you or suggests that these wonderful veggie lumps will then taste like french fries (and what's wrong with that?), chaaps do exceedingly well with a mint or tamarind chutney as well.

Pan-Fried Yam Kebabs

Oaler Kebab

Mustard oil	20 ml/1 tbsp
Yam, peeled and sliced thin	500 g/2½ cups

Cumin seeds	10 g/2 tsp
Fresh chilis, chopped	10 g/2 tsp
Ginger, chopped	5 g/1 tsp
Salt	to taste
Coriander leaves, chopped	10 g/2 tsp
Ghee	20 g/1 tbsp

In a heavy-bottomed pan heat the oil. Add the cumin seeds; when they splutter add the sliced yam. Keep stirring, add the green chilis, salt, and ginger and continue cooking for about fifteen minutes until soft. Sprinkle in the chopped coriander leaves.

When the mixture has cooled, process in a food processor or pass through a food mill to become a firm dough-like texture. Knead this thoroughly. Form into golf ball-sized balls, flatten them to an inch thickness and form patties from them in the palms of your hands. Heat a pan and melt the ghee. Place the patties gently into the ghee so as not to break apart, and cook on moderate heat until both sides are golden and crisp. Serve hot with tamarind and mint chutneys. Yields 10–12 patties

Tip: Add crunch to these patties by rolling them in semolina before frying.

Bengali Potato and Poppy-Seed Cutlet
Postor Chop

Poppy seeds	200 g/1 cup
Potatoes, peeled, boiled, and mashed	500 g/2 ½ cups
Coconut, grated	100 g/½ cup
Cumin seeds, soaked in water, then ground to a paste	20 g/1 tbsp
Fresh chilis, chopped	10 g/2 tsp
Salt	to taste
Sugar	10 g/2 tsp
Oil for deep-frying	

Soak about three quarters of the poppy seeds in warm water for about half an hour. Drain the excess water and grind to a thick paste in a food processor

Make a firm mixture of the mashed potatoes, ground poppy seeds, grated coconut, chopped green chili, cumin seed paste, salt, and the sugar. Divide the mixture into golf ball-sized balls.

Flatten each ball to an inch thickness in the palm of your hand and dredge with the remaining poppy seeds. Deep fry the cutlets in hot oil in a steep-sided skillet or a kadhai. When golden, remove to brown paper to drain. Serve hot with a variety of chutneys and pickles.

Savory Lentil and Spinach Fritters
Patta Vadi

This is a really great snack to prepare for a cocktail party. The spicy and crispy factors have universal appeal.

Moong lentils, split/dhuli moong dal	300 g/1 ½ cups
Fresh chilis, chopped	10 g/2 tsp
Spinach leaves, shredded	100 g/½ cup
Coriander leaves, chopped	10 g/2 tsp
Ginger, shredded	5 g/1 tsp
Turmeric	5 g/1 tsp
Salt	to taste
Oil	to deep fry
Chaat masala (see page 49)	a pinch

Rinse the lentils and soak them in warm water for half an hour or more. Drain and process them in a food processor to form a smooth paste.

Mix the green chilis, spinach, coriander, ginger, turmeric, and salt into the lentil paste. Bring the oil to frying heat in a deep skillet or a kadhai (Indian wok).

Wet your hands with water to prevent sticking. Drop small portions of the batter into the hot oil. (Or, use two spoons, in the manner of preparing "drop" cookies.) On medium heat, stir gently, once or twice, with a slotted spoon until the fritters are crisp. Remove with the slotted spoon and allow to drain on absorbent kitchen towels or brown paper. Sprinkle with chaat masala. Serve immediately with mint chutney. These are eaten with one's hands.

Tip: You can add your personal touch to these dumplings by varying the flavors. Try fenugreek leaves, crushed black peppercorns, chili flakes, basil, chopped carrots, or finely chopped string beans in the mix.

Tangy Potato Salad with Tamarind and Date-Flavored Chutney
Aloo chaat

Potatoes, peeled and boiled, cut into cubes	150 g/¾ cup
Tomatoes, chopped	20 g/1 tbsp
Coriander leaves, chopped	5 g/1 tsp
Onions, chopped	10 g/2 tsp
Ginger, shredded	5 g/1 tsp
Fresh chilis, chopped	1
Salt	to taste
Chaat masala (see page 49)	5 g/1 tsp

For the dressing

Tamarind pulp	10 g/2 tsp
Lemon juice	5 ml/1 tsp
Cumin seeds	a pinch
Oil	5 ml/1 tsp
Palm sugar/Cane sugar/Honey	10g/2 tsp

Boil together all the ingredients for the dressing with a pinch of salt and 50ml/¼ cup water until the sauce coats the back of a spoon. Strain and refrigerate to chill.

Toss together the potatoes, tomatoes, coriander leaves, onions, ginger, fresh chilis, salt, and chaat masala. Add the dressing and continue to toss. Check, and adjust salt, if required. Serve chilled.

Vegetable Fritters

Vegetable Pakodas

Pakodas, often referred to as pakoras or bhajiyas, are available in various styles across India. Busy sidewalks are crowded even further with large carts with a glass-fronted display cabinet and a stove mounted beneath a large pan of oil of questionable age and origin. There is an unending flow of buyers who walk away with newspaper-wrapped packets of these freshly fried savories; the owners of the carts work at a frantic pace to fry up these fritters that keep disappearing. Following is a recipe I recommend you fry up in fresher oil. The measurements are approximate as these are chunks of vegetable and cheese that are coated and deep fried.

Onions, peeled and cut into petals	50g/½ cup
Green pepper, cut into largish cubes	50g/½ cup
Paneer, cut into sticks	50g/½ cup
Green chilis, cut in half and seeds removed	5 chilis; 10 pieces
Spinach leaves, carefully rinsed to remove sand, whole or torn for dipping into batter	1 bunch
Oil	to deep fry

For the batter

Bengal gram flour	100 g/½ cup
Chili powder	10 g/2 tsp
Turmeric	10 g/2 tsp
Salt	to taste
Baking soda	a pinch

In a bowl whisk together the gram flour, chili powder, turmeric, salt, baking soda, and enough water to make a thick batter of coating consistency.

Heat the oil in a kadhai or heavy, deep-sided pot, or a wok. Dip the vegetables individually in the batter until they are completely coated. Lower them carefully into the hot oil and fry until evenly golden and done. A wide (6 in" round) Chinese fry dip works to put them in as well as to take them out. Drain on paper toweling or brown paper. Serve hot with mint and tamarind chutneys.

Tips: This recipe calls for halved chilis, deseeded. Traditionally whole chilis are fried in the batter. Many folks here in India are really into spicy!

Mixing a couple of teaspoons of cornstarch into the batter gives a much crisper texture and finish to the pakoras.

Fried Lentil Dumplings Steeped in Yogurt

Dahi Vada

These yogurt-steeped lentil dumplings are absolutely delicious. Their sweet, spicy, and tangy tastes combine to give your taste buds a real treat. They are available at every 'chaat' vendor, whose numbers dot the crowded streets of every city in India. It is best to eat during the summer months, when its cooling effects are most realized.

White Urad dal	200 g/1 cup
Cumin seeds, roasted/Jeera	a pinch
Fresh chilis, chopped	2
Ginger, chopped	5 g/1 tsp
Mint leaves, chopped	3 g/½ tsp
Yogurt, whipped	400g/2 cups
Sugar	5 g/1 tsp
Cumin powder, roasted	5 g/1 tsp
Chili powder	5 g/1 tsp
Chaat masala (see page 49)	5 g/1 tsp
Mint chutney (see page 187)	as required
Tamarind chutney	as required
Salt	to taste
Oil	to deep fry

Rinse the lentils thoroughly. Soak them in water for six hours or more. Drain and process the lentils to a smooth paste in a food processor.

In a bowl, combine the lentil paste, cumin seeds, chopped green chilis, chopped ginger, chopped mint leaves, and a bit of salt. Form small dumplings in your hand and deep-fry them until they are golden. Remove them from the oil with a slotted spoon to drain on absorbent paper toweling or on brown paper. Soak the dumplings in salted lukewarm water for about ten minutes to soften them.

Whisk the yogurt with the sugar, roasted cumin powder, chili powder, and a bit of salt. Taste and adjust the seasoning, if required. Place it in the refrigerator to chill.

Squeeze the lentil dumplings to drain off excess water. Place them in a serving bowl and pour the whipped yogurt mixture over them. Sprinkle on the chaat masala, mint and tamarind chutneys, and the chopped coriander. Serve chilled.

Steamed Gram Flour Savories
Khaman Dhokla

Chana dal	200 g/1 cup
Fresh chilis, stems removed	10 g/2 tsp
Ginger, peeled	20 g/1 tbsp
Oil	40 ml/2 tbsp
Asafoetida	a pinch
Baking soda	3 g/½ tsp
Salt	to taste

For the tempering (see page 40)

Oil	10 ml/2 tsp
Mustard seeds	a pinch
Cumin seeds	a pinch
Red chilis, dried whole	2
Curry leaves	a pinch
Coriander leaves, chopped	5 g

Soak the lentils in water for at least six hours. Drain, and grind them in a food processor to a coarse paste. Put in a warm place to ferment for about eight hours. Grind the ginger and fresh chilis to a paste in a food processor. Add this to the fermented batter along with the oil, salt, asafoetida, baking soda, and enough water to make a thick batter. When the mixture froths, whisk it briefly and gently pour it into greased molds, or into a greased baking pan such that its depth will be about one inch. Place the batter into the molds or pans, as you have chosen, in a preheated steamer for about twenty minutes (see page 41 about steaming). Remove from the molds and set aside to cool.

For the tempering, heat the oil, and add the cumin, mustard, dried red chilis, and curry leaves. When the spices crackle, drizzle the mixture over the steamed dhoklas using a ladle or similar device. Sprinkle on the coriander leaves and serve warm with chutneys.

Carom Seed Flavored Crisps
Matri

These are thick triangular, layered, savory crisps served with tea in the tiny tea shacks that line Indian streets. One dips these crisps into the cup of tea to soften them, adding a flavor contrast even before one takes a first bite.

White flour	200 g/1 cup
Oil	20 ml/1 tbsp
Carom seeds	3 g/½ tsp
Baking soda	3 g/½ tsp
Black peppercorns	5 g/1 tsp
Salt	to taste
Oil	to deep fry

Knead together the flour, salt, ajwain, soda and enough warm water to make a firm, smooth dough. Divide the dough into golf-ball-sized balls and roll them out to the thickness of a nickel. Create flat discs with approximately a six inch diameter. Fold them in half and then half again to form a rounded triangular shape. Place three black peppercorns in the center and roll out again to form a thickness of about a third of an inch while retaining the rounded triangular shape. With a fork, prick deeply on one side and set aside.

Continue similarly until all the dough has been used.

Heat the oil and gently fry, turning as necessary, until the savories are crisp. Remove with a slotted spoon to drain on paper toweling.

Matri can be stored in airtight containers for a few weeks.

Plain Dosa

Sada Dosa

Southern India's answer to the crepe.

Rice	200 g/1 cup
Urad dal	100 g/½ cup
Channa dal	100 g/½ cup
Fenugreek seeds/methi dana	a pinch
Oil	20 ml/1 tbsp
Salt	to taste
Butter or oil for frying	20 g/1 tbsp

Rinse the rice and the lentils until the water runs clear. Soak the rice, the lentils, and the fenugreek seeds in a bowl, in enough water to cover for at least six hours. Add sufficient water as it is absorbed.

Drain and process the mix in a food processor to a smooth, thick paste. Set aside covered, in a cool place, for at least six hours to ferment.

Heat a flat, non-stick griddle pan. Rub the surface with butter or oil to leave a thin coating. Ladle batter onto the center of the pan using the ladle in a circular motion in order to spread the batter into the shape of a thin, round pancake about the same diameter as the pan. After partly cooked and the surface is set, drizzle a bit of butter onto the top and continue to fry the dosa until the bottom is golden and crisp. Do not turn. This is traditionally served hot with coconut chutneys (see page 188) or sambhar (see page 198).

Semolina Dosa

Rawa Dosa

Semolina	200 g/1 cup
White flour	100 g/½ cup
Rice flour	100 g/½ cup
Fresh chilis, chopped	3
Onions, finely chopped	50 g/¼ cup

Ginger, chopped	5 g/1 tsp
Coriander leaves, chopped	5 g/1 tsp
Curry leaves, shredded	5g/1 tsp
Salt	to taste
Cumin seeds, roasted and crushed	a pinch
Clarified butter/ghee or oil	20 g/1 tbsp

In a bowl, mix the semolina, white flour, rice flour, chilis, onions, ginger, coriander leaves, curry leaves, salt, and cumin.

Whisk in sufficient water to make a thin milk-like consistency batter.

Heat up a non-stick flat griddle plate. Rub the surface with butter or oil to leave a thin coating.

Stirring the batter with a ladle, pour some on the heated cooking surface and spread it with the ladle using a circular motion from the inside outward to create a pancake/crepe a little smaller than the size of the pan. Cook on medium to high heat until the underside is crisp and golden. Do not turn, as the heat will penetrate and cook both sides. Remove from pan and serve hot with chutneys.

Raitas

Raitas came from a subordinate position in the Indian meal. Working their way into prominence, they have become one of the most widely known accompaniments on the Indian table.

A raita was simply just flavored yogurt served with rich spice-laden biryanis. Their sharp, contrasting flavors and an ability to cut through the oils that accompany many dishes soon attracted the attention of connoisseurs. The acid in the yogurt helps to cut through the grease and fat in a dish, making it a winning combination

As the raita-loving community expanded, their flavor, types, and complexity increased. From mono-ingredient-flavored raitas, the demand for originality kept many chefs busy concocting and pounding their spice mixes in the quiet of the night, preserving their secrets from rivals.

As this can only be an introduction, I must set aside the more complex raitas in order to make you familiar with those that have universal appeal.

Raitas are now most often served as a relish or as a dip for savories.

Here's a secret: While many Indians will scorn the addition of sugar, it helps to round off the flavor of a raita. The addition of sugar ensures that the dish will not carry the sharp acidic taste of the yogurt, but a much-mellowed, rounder flavor. The purpose of sweetening it is akin to eating roast pork with applesauce or turkey with cranberries

Basic Raita
Yogurt Dip

This is the super-basic raita recipe. Its universal appeal makes it the perfect accompaniment to biryanis, kebabs, and savories.

Yogurt, thick	100 g/½ cup
Sugar	5 g/1 tsp
Salt	a pinch

Coriander leaves, chopped	5 g/1 tsp
Mint leaves, chopped	5 g/1 tsp
Cucumber, deseeded and chopped	5 g/1 tsp
Tomatoes, deseeded and chopped	10 g/2 tsp
Chili powder	a pinch
Cumin powder, roasted	5 g/1 tsp

Whisk the yogurt with the salt, sugar, chili powder, and cumin powder. Add the rest of the ingredients, taste and adjust seasoning, if required. Can be served immediately or kept chilled for a time, which will improve its flavor.

Tip: To deseed a cucumber, cut the cucumber lengthwise and run a melon baller, vegetable scoop or spoon on the inside from the top down.

Tip: To deseed tomatoes, cut the tomato into quarters, lay the pieces skin side down on a cutting board and slide a sharp knife between the flesh and the seeds and cut the seeds away.

Pineapple Raita

Ananas ka Raita

Pineapple, chopped	100 g/½ cup
Yogurt	400 g/2 cups
Cumin powder, roasted	a pinch
Chili powder	a pinch
Salt	to taste
Oil	20 ml/1 tbsp
Dried red chilis	2
Mustard seeds	a pinch
Curry leaves	a sprig
Coriander leaves, chopped	3 g/½ tsp

Whisk the yogurt in a bowl with the cumin powder, chili powder, and salt until it is smooth. Separately heat the oil, add the chilis, mustard seeds, and curry leaves. When the seeds crackle pour the entire mixture over the yogurt. Add the chopped pineapple and coriander leaves. Stir a few times until it is evenly mixed. Taste and adjust seasoning, if required. Serve.

Asafoetida and Garlic Flavored Raita
Burhani raita

Yogurt	400 g/2 cups
Oil	10 ml/½ tbsp
Asafoetida	5 g/1 tsp
Garlic, peeled and sliced	5 g/1 tsp
Shallots, finely sliced	20 g/1 tbsp
Dried red chilis	2
Salt	to taste
Coriander leaves, chopped	5 g/1 tsp

Whisk the yogurt until smooth and airy and set aside.

Heat the oil in a heavy-bottomed pan. Add the asafoetida and garlic and simmer on low heat until the garlic softens. Add the shallots and chilis and continue to stir on low heat until the shallots turn soft. Add the entire mixture to the yogurt along with the salt and coriander leaves. Stir until all the ingredients are evenly mixed. Adjust the seasoning, if required, before serving.

Spinach and Scallion Raita
Palak aur Hara Pyaaz ka Raita

Yogurt	400 g/2 cups
Ginger, grated	10 g/2 tsp
Green chilis, chopped	5 g/1 tsp
Cumin seed powder, roasted	3 g/½ tsp
Mint leaves, shredded	5 g/1 tsp
Salt	to taste
Sugar	a pinch
Spinach, young leaves, (sold bagged as baby spinach) rinsed and trimmed of their stalks	60g/¼ cup
Scallion, chopped	20g/1 tbsp

Whisk the yogurt with ginger, green chilis, cumin, mint, salt, and sugar. Finely shred the spinach leaves and add to the yogurt along with the scallions. Stir until all the ingredients are evenly mixed. Adjust seasonings as desired.

Allow the raita to sit in the refrigerator for at least twenty minutes for the flavors to meld before serving.

Paneer

Paneer is among the few indigenous cheeses in all of Asia. Although its form and texture resembles cheeses that are known in the West, paneer does not melt at normal cooking temperatures and is not aged, but used fresh. Because the milk is curded without the use of rennet, which is derived from animals, it is truly a vegetarian cheese.

Paneer is made from milk that is curded using acid (most often, lime juice) to separate the curds. The resultant protein masses are strained out and pressed in a mold to help them to stick together to form a block. This block may then be sliced or cut into cubes depending on the dish in preparation.

A softer version of this cheese is prepared without pressing or molding. Instead the cheese is kneaded to form a fluffier, softer cheese which is used in the preparation of desserts.

Although the product originated in India, it was made popular by the Mughal invaders who ruled over most of India in the Middle-Ages.

Paneer, an unsalted cheese, readily accepts flavors and stands up well to prolonged marination. It absorbs the flavors from the dish of which it becomes part, so earlier salting is unnecessary to its addition to a dish.

Paneer is a major source of protein for Indian vegetarians who adhere to a strict lacto-vegetarian diet.

While easy to prepare at home, it is available at most Asian stores.

Homemade Paneer.

I often hear from people that factory-prepared paneer is "too modern" or "characterless." Indeed, nothing can replace the fresh, creamy texture of homemade, home-pressed paneer. Although the method (unchanged since ancient times) takes a little effort, it gets easier after a few times. After making your own, purchase some commercial paneer and compare. Adding to the pleasure of your efforts, you'll find there's no comparison.

Only the milk solids and fats are retained; the residual liquid, the whey, is discarded (or you may freeze it until you have enough to make ricotta). Two quarts of whole milk will yield almost a pound of paneer. Interesting variations may be created by adding ingredients such as carom seeds and turmeric to the milk during the processing.

Whole milk	1 liter/1 quart
Lemon or lime juice	40 ml/2 tbsp

Slowly bring the milk to a boil, stirring continuously to prevent burning. Remove from the heat and add the lemon juice slowly while stirring continuously. When the milk curdles, and the solid matter (curd) floats to the top, stop stirring and allow it to stand for about fifteen minutes. Drain through a cheesecloth so the curds are retained. Squeeze, slowly, a few times to more fully remove the liquid. Wrap tightly and place the cheesecloth bundle on a flat surface with a weight atop it so that the remaining whey will drain away. A bowl or a pot full of water can be used as a weight.

After half an hour or more, remove the weight, unwrap, and cut it into desired pieces.

Although paneer is best used fresh, it keeps well under refrigeration for three to five days.

A simpler alternative method to pressing: After its initial draining and, this time, only a *light* squeezing, tie the cheese in its cheese cloth and hang it from the sink faucet, allowing the cheese to drain overnight. This creates a fluffy cheese that has a lighter texture as compared to the pressed version.

Tip: Add spices such as turmeric, chili flakes or carom seeds to the milk to create flavored paneer

Paneer Simmered with Cream and Black Peppercorns
Paneer Badaami Kali Mirch

Oil or ghee	20 ml/1 tbsp
Cinnamon sticks	2 pieces, about 2–3 inches in length
Cloves	4 buds
Green cardamom	6 pods
Cumin seeds	a pinch

Onions, chopped	150 g/¾ cup
Garlic paste	10 g/2 tsp
Ginger, shredded	10 g/2 tsp
Fresh chilis, chopped	10 g/2 tsp
Tomatoes, chopped	40 g/2 tbsp
Paneer cut into cubes	500 g/2½ cups
Salt	to taste
Cream	50 ml/¼ cup
Black peppercorns, crushed	20 g/1 tbsp
Almonds, blanched, peeled and chopped	40 g/2 tbsp
Coriander leaves, chopped	5 g/1 tsp

Heat the oil in a heavy-bottomed pan, adding the cinnamon, cardamom, cloves, and cumin seeds. When the spices crackle, add the chopped onions and cook until they are golden. Add the garlic and the green chilis and cook until the garlic begins to change color. Add the tomatoes and simmer until they turn soft and pulpy. Keep stirring to prevent the mixture from sticking to the bottom.

Add the paneer and stir on high heat. Sprinkle in a bit of salt and continue to stir for a minute longer. Pour in the cream and the crushed peppercorns. Simmer until the gravy is reduced to the desired thickness. Add the chopped almonds; taste and adjust seasoning, if neccessary. Serve hot, garnished with chopped coriander leaves.

Crumbled Paneer with Spices

Paneer Bhurji

I maintain and stoutly defend this to be the best treatment ever discovered for the use of paneer. Fresh cheese, with its unique texture and taste, provides a versatility that could probably not be attempted with any other ingredient.

Oil	20 ml/1 tbsp
Cumin seeds	a pinch
Onions, chopped	50 g/¼ cup
Fresh chilis, chopped	10 g/2 tsp
Paneer, grated	300 g/1 ½ cup

Turmeric	10 g/2 tsp
Salt	to taste
Tomatoes, chopped	50 g/¼ cup
Coriander leaves, chopped	5 g/1 tsp
Juice of one lemon	

Heat the oil in a heavy-bottomed pan and add the cumin seeds; when they crackle, add the chopped onions and green chilis. Stir on medium heat until the onions are soft; add the paneer cheese, turmeric and salt. Continue to stir to prevent the spices from sticking to the bottom and burning. Add the tomatoes and simmer until they are pulpy. Taste and adjust the seasoning if necessary. Finish with the chopped coriander leaves. Sprinkle on the lemon juice and serve hot.

The consistency of the result will be that of soft, scrambled eggs. Consider topping a naan with this and bringing it to heat in a 450-degree oven for Indian pizza!

Served simply as a side with rice and dal, the result is transformational.

Tip: When paneer is pressed well during its making, it will be firm enough to stand up to grating. If it's too soft, crumbled paneer will do fine for this dish.

Paneer Tossed with Peppers

Paneer Shimla Mirch

Shimla mirch is the Indian term for bell peppers. These were originally grown in Himachal Pradesh. It's name translates to mean chilis from Shimla. Shimla is the capital of the state of Himachal Pradesh. Also pronounced Simla, it was the summer retreat for the British during the days of the Raj. A very important treaty between India and Pakistan known as the Simla accord was signed there.

Oil	20 ml/1 tbsp
Cumin seeds	3 g/½ tsp
Coriander seeds, lightly crushed	5 g/1 tsp
Garlic, sliced	10 g/2 tsp
Onions, cut into cubes	75 g/⅓ cup
Paneer, cut into cubes	250 g/1 ¼ cup

Tomatoes, diced	75 g/⅓ cup
Tomatoes ground to a puree	200 g/1 cup
Fresh chilis, chopped	10 g/2 tsp
Turmeric–	5 g/1 tsp
Salt	to taste
Ginger, shredded	5 g/1 tsp
Bell pepper, diced	150 g/¾ cup
Coriander leaves, chopped	5 g/1 tsp

Heat the oil in a heavy-bottomed pan. Add the cumin and coriander seeds. When they splutter, add the onions and cook until they are soft. Add the garlic. When it begins to change color add the paneer. Stir gently on medium heat for about two minutes. Add the tomatoes, ground tomatoes, green chilis, turmeric and a bit of salt. Simmer on low heat until the tomatoes are pulpy and the sauce begins to thicken. Add the ginger and peppers. Taste and adjust the seasoning, if necessary, and add water if the sauce is too thick. Finish off with the coriander leaves and serve hot with rice or breads

Tip: Use a variety of colored peppers to create a colorful dish.

Curried Paneer Stuffed with Pistachios
Paneer Shahi Korma

Each succeeding Mughal emperor sought to immortalize himself not by great conquests alone, but also by patronizing the arts—including those culinary.

The royal chefs were fiercely competitive with each other in developing and refining recipes for the pleasure of their masters. This dish was originally prepared with chicken, but adapted to paneer to promote the acceptance of their vegetarian courtiers.

Paneer blocks	800 g/4 cups
Poppy seeds	40 g/2 tbsp
Cashew nuts, roughly crushed	40 g/2 tbsp
Ginger, peeled	5 g/1 tsp
Fresh chilis	2
Paneer, grated	50 g/¼ cup

Pistachios, lightly crushed	50 g/¼ cup
Coriander leaves, chopped	5 g/1 tsp
Almonds, sliced	20 g/1 tbsp
Garlic, peeled	4 cloves
Ghee	20 g/1 tbsp
Cinnamon stick	1 piece, about 2–3 inches in length
Green cardamom–	4 pods
Cloves	4 buds
Onions, sliced	40 g/2 tbsp
Turmeric–	5 g/1 tsp
Yogurt, whipped	100 g/½ cup
Cream	40 ml/2 tbsp
Salt	to taste

Cut the paneer blocks into pieces that are two inches square and an inch thick. Place each slice flat. With a sharp knife, gently cut three fourths of the way into the side of each slice to form a "pocket" Gently squeeze open the pocket and rub a bit of salt on the inside surface. Leave in a cool place for ten minutes.

Soak the poppy seeds and crushed cashew nuts in warm water for ten minutes and process them to a fine paste with the ginger and green chilis. Reserve for later use.

Mix together the grated paneer, crushed pistachios, salt, and half the coriander leaves; divide this into four equally sized balls. Gently open the pockets and stuff the paneer slices with the flavored mix and one garlic clove each.

Heat the ghee in a heavy-bottomed pan. Add the cinnamon, cardamom, and cloves. When the cardomom puffs up, add the sliced onions and cook them gently until they are golden. Add the poppy seed paste and stir on medium heat for five minutes so that the raw taste of the poppy seeds disappears. Incorporate the turmeric, salt and yogurt. Then gently place the stuffed cottage cheese slices, continuing to simmer for ten minutes. Add water if necessary.

When the gravy has gotten quite thick, add the cream and almonds and bring to a boil for a minute. Taste and adjust the seasoning if necessary. Remove from heat, garnish with the coriander leaves, and serve hot.

Cauliflower

Many consider the cauliflower the most beautiful of all vegetables. I agree. A creamy white cauliflower with its intricately interlocked florets flanked by beautiful, tender green leaves—that is something really beautiful.

Cauliflower is from the family 'Brassicaceae' which is related to broccoli and brussels sprouts. Usually, only the creamy white head, often referred to as 'white curd' is eaten, but in some parts of India a separate dish is made with the leaves.

Although most cauliflower is white, there are a variety of colors available. Orange cauliflower is available in most parts of North America and the purple variety was first found in Italy.

Cauliflower is used sometimes as a potato substitute. It has substantial body but not the high starch/carbohydrate levels. Something so very good is hard to ignore. Let's cook with it.

Cauliflower Simmered with Yogurt and Carom Seed
Ajwaini Gobi

Oil	20 ml/1 tbsp
Carom seeds/ajwain	5 g/1 tsp
Cauliflower florets	400 g/2 cups
Turmeric–	10 g/2 tsp
Fresh chilis,chopped	10 g/2 tsp
Salt	to taste
Yogurt	70 g/⅓ cup
Sugar	5 g/1 tsp
Coriander leaves, chopped	5 g/1 tsp

Heat the oil in a heavy-bottomed pan. Add the carom seeds. When they crackle, add the cauliflower, turmeric, green chilis, and a bit of salt. Toss on high heat until the florets appear translucent. Add the yogurt and reduce the heat.

Cover with a lid and simmer for about fifteen minutes, until the cauliflower is tender, taking care to stir occasionally. If the liquid evaporates before the florets are tender, add more water. When they are tender and the sauce coats them, stir in the coriander leaves. Taste and adjust the seasoning, if required. Serve hot.

Stir Fried Potatoes and Cauliflower with Cumin
Aloo gobi masala

Oil	20 ml/1 tbsp
Cumin seeds/jeera	5 g/1 tsp
Potatoes peeled and diced	150 g/¾ cup
Cauliflower, cut into tiny florets	200 g/1 cup
Garlic, chopped	5 g/1 tsp
Ginger, finely shredded	a pinch
Turmeric–	10 g/2 tsp
Fresh chilis, chopped	10 g/2 tsp
Tomatoes, chopped	70 g/⅓ cup
Salt	to taste
Sugar	a pinch
Coriander leaves, chopped	5 g/1 tsp

Heat the oil in a heavy-bottomed pan. Add the cumin seeds. When they crackle, add the potatoes, cauliflower, chopped garlic, and a bit of salt. Stir on medium heat until the vegetables appear translucent. Add the turmeric and ginger. Stir for a minute. Add the tomatoes and the green chilis. Simmer for ten minutes, stirring occasionally or until the tomatoes are pulpy. Add the sugar, taste, and adjust the seasoning, if required. When the vegetables are cooked through, add the coriander leaves and serve hot.

Cauliflower Florets Tossed with Bell Peppers
Gobi Benarasi

If you substitute the cauliflower with mushrooms, this dish is known as Khumb Simia Mirch.

Oil	20 ml/1 tbsp
Carom seeds/ajwain	a pinch
Shallots, chopped	70 g/⅓ cup
Cauliflower florets	500 g/2 ½ cups
Turmeric	5 g/1 tsp
Fresh tomatoes, pureed	150 g/¾ cup
Ginger, shredded	10 g/2 tsp
Fresh chilis, chopped	10 g/2 tsp
Sugar	a pinch
Green bell pepper, sliced	50 g/¼ cup
Scallions, shredded	20 g/1 tbsp
Salt	to taste
Juice of one lemon	
Coriander leaves, chopped	5 g/1 tsp

Heat the oil in a heavy-bottomed pan and add the carom seeds. When they splutter, add the shallots and stir them on medium heat until they are transparent. Add the cauliflower and sprinkle on the turmeric and a bit of salt. Stir a few times and add the pureed tomatoes and a bit of water. Simmer until the cauliflower is almost tender and most of the liquid has been absorbed.

Add the ginger, green chilis, sugar, bell pepper, scallions, and toss until the cauliflower is tender. Stir in the lemon juice and coriander leaves. Taste and adjust the seasoning, if required, and serve hot.

Tip: Turmeric burns easily, potentially spoiling a dish. This is why it is not added while roasting other spices.

Carrots

The carrot is a plant that has no doubt seen the most controversy, political intrigue, debauchery, and odd history in its supposed five thousand years of cultivation. It was not always the succulent, brightly colored taproot we now so easily obtain at markets. It used to be an ugly, skinny, acrid-tasting, dark purple or black wild plant that no one wanted to eat!

Its journey of transformation began in what is part of Afghanistan, where it first grew over five thousand years ago. It traveled through the subcontinent, reaching Pakistan and India. Arab traders spread the seed to Asia, the Middle-East and Africa. There are hieroglyphics in ancient Egypt that show a plant resembling a carrot dating back to 2,000 B.C.

Carrots were used as an aphrodisiac in that they closely resemble other roots like Mandrake and Ginseng that are used for this purpose. Ancient Indian texts name them as a treatment for impotence. Ancient physicians Galen, Pliny the Elder, and Hippocrates, the father of modern medicine, marveled at the qualities of the carrot.

Carrot seeds were found in the ancient tombs of pharaohs. Caligula, the crazed Roman emperor, is said to have served a banquet composed only of carrot dishes so that he could observe his guests becoming more and more aroused.

Because carrots were not then pleasing to the taste, only their fragrant flowers, leaves and the seeds were used as food. That they were ugly dark purple or black added to the difficulties of cooking them because they colored whatever was cooked with them. Dutch botanists in the 15th Century cross-bred the carrot with several wild red varieties to create the orange color that we know today; this was done to honor the ruling house of Orange (Oranje)that governed Holland at that time.

Carrots are a nutritional goldmine and are often prescribed to patients who are deficient in Vitamin A. The high level of beta carotene (which gives the vegetable its color) converts to Vitamin A soon after as it is eaten. Carrots are also rich in Vitamins B, C, D and E, thiamine, folic acid and minerals.

Carrot and Coconut Stir-Fry
Carrot Poriyal

Poriyals can be made with numerous star ingredients. One can make a green bean poriyal, an okra poriyal, or a cauliflower poriyal. You get the idea. Poriy'all hearts into this and come up with your own favorite--corn, mushroom, whatever. However, I'd stop at jellybean poriyal.

Coconut oil	20 ml/1 tbsp
Mustard seeds	a pinch
Curry leaves	a sprig
Dried red chilis, halved	2 chilis
Black lentils/urad dal	3g/½ tsp
Split Bengal gram/chana dal	3g/½ tsp
Asafoetida/hing	a pinch
Turmeric	a pinch
Carrots, peeled and diced	500g/2 ½ cups
Salt	to taste
Sugar	a pinch
Fresh coconut, grated	30g/2 tbsp
Coriander leaves, chopped	5g/1 tsp

Heat the oil in a heavy-bottomed pan. Add the mustard, curry leaves, and dried chilis. When the seeds splutter, add the lentils and asafoetida. Stir gently until they change color and then add the carrots, turmeric, salt, sugar and 80 ml/1/3 cup of water. Simmer, stirring occasionally, until most of the liquid has been absorbed and the carrots are tender. Sprinkle in the grated coconut and coriander leaves and stir so that they are evenly mixed. Taste and adjust seasoning if required. Serve hot.

Tip: If fresh coconut is not available, canned or desiccated coconut can be used.

Spicy Carrot and Coriander Stew
Gajar dhaniwal masala

Carrots, diced	400 g/2 cups
Oil	20 ml/1 tbsp
Cumin seeds	a pinch
Onions, peeled	70 g/⅓ cup
Garlic, peeled	10 g/2 tsp
Ginger, peeled	5 g/1 tsp
Coriander leaves	40 g/2 tbsp
Fresh chilis	10 g/2 tsp
Tomatoes, cut into quarters	150 g/equivalent to ¾ cup
Salt	to taste
Sugar	a pinch
Mint leaves	5 g/1 tsp

In a food processor, combine the onions, garlic, ginger, coriander leaves, and green chilis and process to a smooth paste.

Heat the oil in a heavy-bottomed pan. Add the cumin seeds. When the seeds crackle, add the paste and the carrots and stir over low heat for a few minutes or until the mixture begins to thicken and the carrots are almost tender. Add the tomatoes, salt, and sugar and stir until the tomatoes turn soft. Taste and adjust the seasoning, if required. Finish with the mint leaves. Serve hot.

Tip: Most of the liquid in this stew is derived from the ground onions and the tomatoes. If necessary, a bit of water can be sprinkled in to aid in the cooking.

Green Peas

Peas are an ancient legume that probably emerged in food preparation about seven thousand years ago along with barley and wheat. The first appearance may have been in parts of Syria where it was allowed to mature, dry and then used much as lentils are today.

Around the seventeenth century immature ("baby") peas were eaten fresh. It became a fad that at one point bordered on hysteria . However, the dishes produced were not worthy of this beautiful vegetable. The peas were merely drenched in hot butter with some mint and slapped onto the table.

In India, fresh peas are available only during winter because the crops do not survive our hot summers. Frozen peas have eliminated the need for us to wait for winter to eat this wonderful-tasting vegetable.

Peas are a great source of Vitamins A, C, thiamine, iron, phosphorous, and folate which is the anionic form of folic acid. It is also one of the largest fresh vegetable sources of protein.

We have moved on from the time of dribbling butter on peas as the following recipes will demonstrate.

Green Peas and Paneer Simmered in Spicy Tomato Gravy

Matar Paneer

Paneer, cut into cubes	70 g/⅓ cup
Green peas	50 g/¼ cup
Oil	20 ml/1 tbsp
Onions, chopped	100 g/½ cup
Tomatoes, pureed	100 g/½ cup
Tomato paste	10 g/2 tsp
Red chili paste (see page 20)	5 g/1 tsp
Turmeric	a pinch

Dried fenugreek leaves/kasturi methi	5 g/1 tsp
Green cardamom	3 pods
Bay leaf	1
Chaat masala (see page 49)	a pinch
Sugar	a pinch
Coriander leaves, chopped	5 g/1 tsp

Heat the oil in a heavy-bottomed pan. Add the chopped onions. Cook until the onions are golden brown. Add the tomato paste and stir for a few minutes to prevent the mix from sticking to the bottom. Add the pureed tomatoes, chili paste, and turmeric, stir and simmer for a few minutes with the cardamom pods and the bay leaf.

When the sauce begins to thicken, add some water and the paneer and green peas. Simmer for about ten minutes. Stir occasionally, taste and adjust seasoning, if required. When the gravy has thickened and coats the cheese cubes, add the fenugreek, chaat masala, and chopped fresh coriander. Sprinkle in the sugar, taste again and adjust, if required. Serve hot.

Green Peas and Fenugreek Leaves in a Creamy Sauce
Methi Matar Malai

I once had an organic garden where I grew my own fenugreek. Financial realities required that I give up my peaceful life of less than plenty, but I will always remember the fragrance and divine taste of garden-fresh ingredients complemented by fresh cream and home-churned butter.

Fenugreek leaves have a delightful bitterish taste that complements the sweetness of green peas. Fresh leaves are flown regularly to the U.S. and are sold at many Indian stores.

Green peas	150 g/¾ cup
Chopped fenugreek leaves	100 g/½ cup
Thick cream	40 g/2 tbsp
Butter or ghee	20 g/1 tbsp
Oil	20 ml/1 tbsp
Cumin seeds	a pinch

Asafoetida/hing	a pinch
Cinnamon sticks	2 pieces, about 2–3 inches in length
Green cardamom	3 pods
Cloves	5 buds
Onions	150 g/¾ cup
Poppy seeds/khuskhus	20 g/1 tbsp
Cashew nuts	20 g/1 tbsp
Green chilis	10 g/2 tsp
Ginger, peeled	10 g/2 tsp
Garlic cloves, peeled	10 g/2 tsp
Yogurt	20 g/1 tbsp
Sugar	10 g/2 tsp
Salt	to taste

Grind the cardamom and cloves to a fine powder, add the cinnamon, and re-serve.

Soak the poppy seeds and cashews in hot water for about ten minutes and process them to a fine paste along with the onions, green chilis, ginger, garlic, and the yogurt.

Soak the fenugreek seeds in hot salted water for ten minutes, drain, rinse in a strainer under running tap water, squeeze out the extra liquid, and set aside.

Heat the oil in a heavy-bottomed pan. Add the cumin and asafoetida. When the seeds crackle, add the poppy seed paste and stir over medium heat for about ten minutes until the paste is golden. Add the green peas, fenugreek leaves, salt, sugar, ground spice powder, cream, and 50 ml/¼ cup of water. Simmer slowly. When the gravy begins to thicken, increase the heat and bring to a boil. Taste and adjust the seasoning, if necessary. Finish off with butter, remove from heat, and serve hot with parathas.

Tip: Dried fenugreek leaves, known as kasturi/qasturi methi cannot be used as a substitute for fresh leaves.

Bitter Melon/Karela

Often called bitter melon, sometimes bitter pear, this vegetable is an acquired taste. It is generally available, fresh, at Chinese markets in the U.S. It was not named bitter by mistake, yet it remains one of the most popular vegetables in Asia, the Caribbean, and parts of Africa.

The fruit has an edible skin. Its texture is crunchy, yet watery—and, again, extremely bitter. It is often used in southeast Asian and Chinese cuisines for the bitter flavor it imparts.

Karela comes in a variety of shapes and sizes. The Indian variety is normally six to eight inches long, tapering at either end, with a shiny green skin that is covered with a series of ridges. The Asian or Chinese variety is slightly longer, with pale green and relatively smoother skin and blunt ends.

While edible, the skin of the bitter melon should be peeled off. Although it is a rather thin skin, it gets chewy upon cooking. The Indian variety of bitter melon has a rough skin that is often scraped off with a sharp knife.

The seeds are especially bitter and must be discarded before cooking. Tender, young fruit is less bitter than the mature ones. It is often necessary to reduce its bitterness, a relatively simple thing to do. Slice them in half lengthwise and scoop out the seeds and the pith that surrounds them. Salt the inside liberally and set them aside for about an hour. Wash off the salt thoroughly and then slice them as required for your dish.

They may be gratinéed, stir-fried, deep-fried, stewed or even stuffed and baked. However you eat it, this wonder is sure to leave a long-lasting impression.

For the less adventurous—if you choose not to use bitter melon, it can be substituted in all recipes with any one of your choice of squashes.

Mangalorean Style Bitter-Melon Curry

Kanchala Gassi

Gassi is a famous curry that originated in what was once a sleepy hamlet in South India. Centuries ago, a series of natural calamities forced the inhabitants to migrate to more promising parts of India. They carried with them just the bare necessities and the recipe for their famous curry. One may use almost any vegetable as the prime ingredient.

Bitter melon/Karela, finely chopped (see instructions for preparation)	400 g/2 cups
Tamarind pulp	40 g/2 tbsp
Palm sugar/jaggery or brown sugar	40 g/2 tbsp
Grated coconut	400 g/2 cups
Dried red chilis	10, or as suits your heat level
Coriander seeds	5 g/1 tsp
Cumin seeds/Jeera	5 g/1 tsp
Urad dal	5 g/1 tsp
Rice grains, raw	5 g/1 tsp
Curry leaves	2 sprigs
Oil	20 ml/1 tbsp
Mustard seeds	a pinch
Garlic cloves, sliced	5 g/1 tsp
Salt	to taste

Salt the bitter melon per the introduction to this section on page 92. Set it aside for half an hour. Afterward, drain the excess water and squeeze the pulp further to extract all moisture that you possibly can. Simmer it in 200 ml (1 cup) of water, with the sugar and the tamarind pulp.

Individually roast the dried chilis, coriander seeds, cumin, lentils, rice, and half the curry leaves and process to a rough paste with the coconut, adding some water if necessary.

Add the spice paste to the simmering karela with a bit of water to thin down the sauce, if necessary. Season with salt and simmer for about ten minutes until the vegetable is cooked through.

Heat oil in a heavy-bottomed pan. Add the remaining curry leaves, mustard seeds, and garlic. When the seeds crackle, pour it over the curry. Stir, taste, and adjust the seasoning, if required. Serve hot.

Tip: Dried curry leaves can substitute for fresh. If you buy a pack of fresh leaves, they will dry on their own and you can use those leaves as required. If you don't have them, it's ok to delete them. They are fragrant, and the reason a curry is called a curry, but they are not absolutely mandatory.

Bitter Melon Hash

Karela Bhate

A Bhate is a traditional Bengali dish. The name means something that has been mashed. The Bengali community uses this as an accompaniment to the main meal and makes several varieties using a combination of ingredients.

Bitter melon, prepared per the introduction on page 92	70 g/⅓ cup
Turmeric	a pinch
Boiled potato, peeled	150/¾ cup
Fresh chilis, chopped	3 g/½ tsp
Mustard oil	10 ml/½ tbsp
Salt	to taste

Cut the melon into small pieces.

Boil for fifteen minutes in salted water to which the turmeric has been added. Remove from heat when the vegetable softens. Drain. Mash the melon while it is still hot.

Add the boiled potato, green chilis, mustard oil, and salt and continue to mash until a homogenous mixture.

Taste and adjust salt, if necessary. Serve at room temperature.

Bitter Melon Stir-Fry

Karela Bhuni

Karela, sliced, prepared in accord with the introduction on page 92	500 g/1.1 lbs
Onions, chopped	125 g/⅝ cup
Cumin seeds/jeera	5 g/1 tsp
Sunflower oil	20 ml/1 tbsp
Salt	to taste
Sugar	5 g/1 tsp
Chili powder	5 g/1 tsp

In a heavy-bottomed pan, heat the oil. When hot, fry the sliced karela until they are golden and crisp. Remove to an absorbent kitchen paper towel. Drain the excess oil.

Heat the remaining oil, stir in the cumin seeds until they crackle. Reduce the heat and add the onions and cook until they are browned. Add salt and chili powder.

Add the sliced karela, stir well, and add the sugar. Toss lightly, check seasoning and serve hot.

Okra

Okra has earned itself praise for being a great tasting vegetable while garnering scorn for its gummy, sticky characteristics.

Okra comes from the Abyssinian Empire which spanned present day Ethiopia, parts of Eritrea, Djibouti and Sudan. Early trading with the Arabs and the Indians spread its use in those countries. Several documents that have survived the middle ages suggest that it was cultivated along the Nile and in India.

Frequent clashes with the Moors moved the crop toward Spain and Portugal. African slave trafficking helped to spread the popularity of this vegetable to the United States where it is regularly cooked, especially in the Southern states.

Before its use as a table vegetable was recognized, okra was used as a thickening agent. As well as being used fresh, it can be dried and prepared as a powder that is used as a thickening agent much like cornstarch and several other starches.

Pickled, deep-fried, steamed, stewed, stir-fried, in tempura—okra will stand up to a great variety of culinary preparations. Okra is best at its young, tender stage; they take on a woody characteristic when they grow older. The skin has a fuzzy, felt-like quality while the inside contains tender, edible seeds. Its long, slender appearance topped with a conical cap earned it the nickname, "lady's finger."

Okra provides large amounts of potassium and calcium along with dietary fiber and vitamins A, B1, B2, B3 and B6.

Remember to wash okra and pat it dry before cutting. If you've not used this vegetable before, do not be put off by its characteristic gumminess.

Okra Tossed with Mangoes
Bhindi Aamwali

Okra, ends trimmed	200 g/1 cup
Oil	40 ml/2 tbsp

Cumin seeds	a pinch
Onions, chopped	50 g/¼ cup
Tomatoes, chopped	70 g/⅓ cup
Ginger, chopped	5 g/1 tsp
Chili powder	5 g/1 tsp
Turmeric	3 g/½ tsp
Mangoes, peeled and chopped	20 g/1 tbsp
Salt	to taste
Coriander leaves, chopped	5 g/1 tsp
Dried mango powder/amchur	a pinch

Heat the oil in a heavy-bottomed pan and fry the okra until they are bright green. Remove from the pan and put aside to drain any excess oil.

Reheat the same oil and add the cumin seeds. When they crackle, add the onions and toss them until they are golden. Add the tomatoes. Reduce the heat to a simmer and stir occasionally until the tomatoes are pulpy. Add the turmeric, chili powder, ginger, and the okra and toss a few times. Add the mangoes, salt, and coriander. Toss until the mixture becomes moist and coats the okra. Finish with the amchur, remove from the heat, taste, and adjust the seasoning, if necessary. Serve.

Spice-Marinated Okra Crisps
Karare Bhindi

Okra, ends trimmed	500 g/1.1 lb
Bengal gram flour	50 g/¼ cup
Chili powder	10 g/2 tsp
Turmeric–	5 g/1 tsp
Carom seeds/ajwain	a pinch
Salt	to taste
Chaat masala (see page 49)	5 g/1 tsp
Oil	to deep fry

Slice the okra lengthwise into long thin strips. Mix together the Bengal gram flour, chili powder, turmeric, carom seeds, salt, and enough water to make it into a thick paste. Gently mix this in with your fingers, coating the okra very carefully, so as not to break them.

Heat the oil and add the batter-marinated okra a little at a time ensuring that they do not clump. Deep fry until they are crisp. Remove with a slotted spoon and place on absorbent kitchen paper toweling or brown paper. Toss them in chaat masala and serve immediately.

Spice-Stuffed Okra in a Tangy Curry Sauce
Bharwaan Bhindi Masala

Okra, ends trimmed	400 g/2 cups
Mustard seeds	5 g/1 tsp
Poppy seeds /Rai–	10 g/2 tsp
Roasted cumin seeds/jeera	5 g/1 tsp
Fresh chilis	3
Raw mango powder/amchur	a pinch
Oil	20 ml/1 tbsp
Carom seeds/Ajwain	3 g/½ tsp
Asafoetida/Hing	a pinch
Onions, chopped	70 g/⅓ cup
Garlic, chopped	5 g/1 tsp
Tomatoes, chopped	50 g/¼ cup
Chili powder	5 g/1 tsp
Turmeric	10 g/2 tsp
Coconut milk	300 ml/1 ½ cup
Green mango flesh, chopped	40 g/2 tbsp
Salt	to taste
Coriander leaves, chopped	5 g/1 tsp

Soak the mustard and poppy seeds in warm water for twenty minutes. Drain and process them to a paste along with the cumin, green chilis, amchur powder, and a bit of salt.

Make a lengthwise slit in the side of the okra and stuff each with some of the paste. Heat the oil in a heavy-bottomed pan and fry the okra until they are bright green. Remove from the oil and drain.

Reheat the previously used pan. Add the carom seeds and asafoetida. When the seeds crackle, add the chopped onions. Gently saute until the onions turn golden, add the garlic and when it changes color, add the tomatoes, chili powder, and turmeric. Simmer until the tomatoes are pulpy. Add the coconut, milk, green mango, and fried okra. Simmer until the okra is tender and cooked through and the sauce is quite thick. Taste and adjust the seasoning, if required. Finish with the coriander leaves and serve hot.

Okra in Yogurt Sauce
Doi Bhindi

Okra, ends trimmed and sliced in half lengthwise	500 g/1 lb
Yogurt	200 g/1 cup
Tomato, chopped	50 g/¼ cup
Ginger, chopped	20 g/1 tbsp
Chili powder	5 g/1 tsp
Turmeric	5 g/1 tsp
Bay leaves	3
Cumin seeds/jeera	5 g/1 tsp
Salt	to taste
Sugar	5 g/1 tsp
Asafoetida/hing	5 g/1 tsp
Ghee	10 g/2 tsp
Mustard oil	40 ml/2 tbsp
Garam masala powder	5 g/1 tsp

Heat the mustard oil and gently fry the okra. Remove and drain on absorbent kitchen toweling or brown paper.

In the previously used pan, add the bay leaves, cumin seeds and asafoetida. When the cumin crackles, add the ginger followed by chili powder, turmeric, and salt.

Whip the yogurt and pour it over the cooked spices. Add the fried okra, the sugar, some salt, and the chopped tomatoes and stir. Add 50 ml/¼ cup water and simmer.

Taste and adjust the seasoning or sugar, if necessary. Finish by drizzling them with ghee and sprinkling on the garam masala.

Okra Cooked in a Bengali Mustard Sauce

Bhindi Jhaal

'Jhaal' is a traditional Bengali preparation that usually has fish simmering in it. From the mid-nineteenth to the turn of the twentieth century, the city saw an influx of Marwari traders who were compelled by their religion to be vegetarians. Not wishing to deprive their new guests of the finer aspects of traditional Bengali hospitality, modifications were made to the recipe to provide the needs of their new vegetarian compatriots.

Okra, ends trimmed	500 g/1.1 lb
Yellow mustard seeds	40 g/2 tbsp
Black mustard seeds	40 g/2 tbsp
Fresh chilis	20 g/1 tbsp
Fresh chilis, slit (see page 29)	3
Mustard oil	40 ml/2 tbsp
Fresh tomatoes, pureed	50 g/¼ cup
Water	50 ml/¼ cup
Turmeric–	20 g/1 tbsp
Chili powder	5 g/1 tsp
Salt	to taste

Soak the mustard seeds for an hour in 50 ml/¼ cup of hot, just-boiled water. Drain and process together to a paste with the green chilis.

Heat the oil in a heavy-bottomed pan. When it begins to smoke, add the okra and fry until the vegetables turn bright green. Remove and drain the excess oil. Sprinkle on some salt and a bit of the chili powder.

Reheat the oil in the same pan and stir in the tomato puree. When it changes color, turning darker, add the mustard paste. Add the water and simmer a moment. Sprinkle on the turmeric and chili powder and continue simmering. When the sauce thickens, add back the fried okra and simmer in the gravy to reheat it. Check seasoning and remove. Serve with steamed rice.

Traditional Goan Okra Curry
Bhindichi Kodi

Okra, washed and ends trimmed	500 g/1.1 lb
Fresh chili, slit (see page 29)	4
Coconut oil	20 ml/1 tbsp
Onion, sliced	50g/¼ cup
Coconut, fresh and grated	500 g/1.1 lb
Coriander seeds	10g/2 tsp
Cumin seeds	5g/1 tsp
Garlic, chopped	10g/2 tsp
Red chillies, dried	10g/2 tsp
Black peppercorns, whole	10g/2 tsp
Turmeric–	10g/2 tsp
Tamarind pulp extract	15ml/1 tbsp
Sliced sun-dried mango flesh /amchoor (optional)	10g/2 tsp
Salt	to taste

Grind together the coconut, coriander seeds, cumin seeds, dried chillies, and turmeric. Add 70 ml / 1/3 cup of lukewarm water and let it stand.

After ten minutes or so, when the coconut has absorbed most of the water, squeeze everything through a muslin/cheese cloth or a fine meshed sieve, reserving the liquid while discarding the coconut mix.

In a thick–bottomed pot, heat the oil. Fry the okra until they are bright green and tender. Remove from the oil with a slotted spoon and reserve.

Reheat the same oil and gently sautee the sliced onion until golden. Add the chopped garlic and stir gently. When the garlic has softened, add the coconut milk extract, the slit green chilis, and the amchoor and bring to heat. Add the tamarind pulp extract, the fried okra, and a pinch of salt. Simmer until the sauce has suitably thickened and the okra is cooked through and tender. Check and adjust seasoning, if necessary.

Potato

The potato is a perennial plant of the deadly nightshade family that is grown for its starchy tuber. The potato originated in Peru where it was first cultivated nearly seven thousand years ago. It is now the world's most widely grown tuber. We owe thanks to the Andeans who allowed the crop to travel to Spain from where it spread to the rest of the world with European colonization.

Potatoes are primarily carbohydrate in the form of starch. There are about twenty six grams of carbohydrate in a medium size potato.

Potatoes contain many vitamins and minerals and, when eaten with the skin, provide dietary fiber. Unlike many other heavily cultivated crops, they contain many of the vitamins required for proper nutrition.

What is wonderful about the potato is its great versatility; it can be prepared in many ways as exhibited in the recipes that follow.

Potatoes vary in the amount of water they contain. The liquid called for in the recipe should be adjusted to account for these differences.

Potatoes Simmered in a Light Curry Sauce

Aloo Rassa

This is the premier basic potato gravy. Its simplicity must not be equated with palate passivity as this sauce provides an earthy sensuality and a taste finish that is wonderfully bright and pleasant.

Small potatoes, peeled	400 g/2 cups
Oil	20 ml/1 tbsp
Cumin seeds	a pinch
Onions, chopped	100 g/½ cup
Garlic, chopped	10 g/2 tsp
Tomatoes, chopped	150 g/¾ cup
Fresh chilis, chopped	10 g/2 tsp

Turmeric	10 g/2 tsp
Palm sugar or Brown sugar	a pinch
Salt	to taste
Coriander leaves, chopped	5 g/1 tsp

Heat the oil in a heavy-bottomed pot. Add the cumin seeds. When they crackle add the chopped onions and stir until the onions are golden. Add the chopped garlic and stir over moderate heat until the garlic softens and is about to change color. Add the potatoes and the turmeric. Increase the heat and cook on high heat until the potatoes appear evenly colored. Add the tomatoes, chopped green chilis, and salt to taste. Simmer until the tomatoes turn pulpy. Add 400 ml (2 cups) of water and simmer until the potatoes are soft and cooked through and the gravy is somewhat thickened. Add the sugar and bring to a boil. Taste and adjust the seasoning, if necessary. Finish with the chopped coriander leaves and serve hot.

Potatoes Steeped in Spiced Tamarind Sauce

Imli Wale Aloo

The original recipe uses honey instead of sugar; using sugar makes the dish vegan. If you prefer the original taste, replace the sugar with an equal amount of honey.

Potatoes, peeled and cut into quarters	400 g/2 cups
Oil	20 ml/1 tbsp
Fennel seeds	5 g/1 tsp
Fresh chilis, chopped	10 g/2 tsp
Turmeric–	5 g/1 tsp
Tamarind pulp	20 g/1 tbsp
Cane sugar or honey	20 g/1 tbsp
Salt	to taste
Coriander leaves, chopped	5 g/1 tsp

Heat the oil in a heavy-bottomed pot. Add the fennel seeds. When they crackle, add the potatoes. Lightly turn and toss the potatoes on high heat until they begin to brown; add the green chilis, turmeric, salt, and the tamarind pulp. Lower the heat. Add 300 ml (1 ½ cups) of water and simmer for approximately twenty minutes until the potatoes are tender and done. Add the sugar or honey and continue to simmer until the gravy thickens and coats the potatoes. Stir in the coriander leaves. Taste and adjust seasoning, if required. Serve hot.

Spicy Potatoes with a Raw Mango Sprinkle

Aloo Chatpate

Thin-skinned small potatoes	400 g/2 cups
Turmeric	10 g/2 tsp
Oil	to deep fry
Oil	20 ml/1 tbsp
Mustard seeds	5 g/1 tsp
Curry leaves	1 sprig
Onions, chopped	50 g/¼ cup
Tomatoes, chopped	100 g/½ cup
Fresh chilis, chopped	5 g/1 tsp
Chili powder	5 g/1 tsp
Raw mango powde/amchur powder	10 g/2 tsp
Salt	to taste
Coriander leaves, chopped	10 g/1 tsp

In salted water to which half the turmeric has been added, parboil the potatoes until they are almost done. Drain and return to pot over low heat to dry them. Once dry, deep fry them in oil until they are crisply browned and golden and cooked through. Remove with a slotted spoon to drain on absorbent kitchen paper toweling or brown paper.

Heat the 20 ml/1 tbsp of oil in a heavy-bottomed pan. Add the mustard seeds and curry leaves. When they crackle, add the onions and toss them until they are golden. Add the tomatoes, green chilis, chopped green chilis, chili powder, and salt. Stir over low heat until the tomatoes are pulpy. Add the potatoes and toss gently until the mixture coats the potatoes. Stir in the coriander leaves and amchur powder, taste and adjust the seasoning, if required. Serve hot.

Potatoes Cooked with Pomegranate Seeds

Aloo Anardana

This dish is sometimes called "Anarkali," named after a woman of legendary beauty, a famous dancer in the court of the great Mughal Emperor Akbar around the middle of the second millennium. Salim, the emperor's son wished to marry Anarkali, but his father forbade this. Salim raised an army against his father and lost. He was given the choice of death or disavowing Anarkali. He chose death. Anarkali, who loved Salim, asked for a single night of pleasure with Salim and her own death in exchange. Akbar, the emperor agreed and toward dawn, when she had to leave, Anarkali drugged the prince to sleep with a laced pomegranate.

The best way to obtain their kernels is to cut a pomegranate in half. Holding the cut side down on your palm, place your hand over a bowl. Slightly cup your palm while gripping the fruit. Hit the skin with a heavy spoon or other implement to loosen the kernels, your cupped hand directing them into the bowl.

Potatoes, peeled and diced	400 g/2 cups
Oil	20 g/1 tbsp
Onions, chopped	150 g/¾ cup
Tomatoes, chopped	200 g/1 cup
Garlic, chopped	20 g/1 tbsp
Ginger, shredded	5 g/1 tsp
Cashew nuts	50 g/¼ cup
Fresh chilis, chopped	10 g/2 tsp
Turmeric–	5 g/1 tsp
Green cardamom–	6 pods
Pomegranate seeds, fresh	50 g/¼ cup
Coriander leaves, chopped	5 g/1 tsp
Salt	to taste

Soak the cashews in warm water for fifteen minutes. Drain and grind them to a fine paste in a food processor or pound them using a mortar and pestle.

Heat the oil in a pot and saute the onions until they are golden. Add the garlic and stir until it changes color. Add the tomatoes and simmer until they turn pulpy. Add the potatoes, green chilis, turmeric, and some salt; stir until the potatoes take on the color of the mixture. Add the cashew paste, cardamom pods, and enough water for the potatoes to continue to simmer until a fairly thick gravy comes together. Taste and adjust the seasoning, if required. Stir in the pomegranate seeds and chopped coriander. Serve hot.

Goan Cashew Nut and Potato Curry
Batate Kajuchi Kodi

Potatoes, peeled and cut into cubes	400 g/2 cups
Oil	20 ml/1 tbsp
Cumin seeds	3 g/½ tsp
Onions, chopped	50 g/¼ cup
Garlic, chopped	5 g/1 tsp
Tomatoes, chopped	50 g/¼ cup
Turmeric	10 g/2 tsp
Fresh chilis, slit (see page 29)	2
Cashew nuts ground to a powder	20 g/1 tbsp
Water-	200 ml/1 cup
Cashew nuts, whole	10 g/2 tsp
Coconut milk	400 ml/2 cups
Salt	to taste
Coriander leaves, chopped	10 g/2 tsp

Heat the oil in a heavy-bottomed pot. Add the cumin seeds. When they crackle, add the onions, and cook until they are golden. Add the chopped garlic and stir until it is soft. Add the tomatoes, turmeric, and a bit of salt. When the tomatoes turn pulpy, add the ground cashews, water, and coconut milk. Simmer until the potatoes are tender and almost done. Add the whole cashews and bring the sauce to a boil, adding water, if necessary. Taste and adjust the seasonings, if required. Reduce until the sauce is suitably thick. Stir in the coriander leaves and serve hot.

Potatoes Tossed with Scallions

Aloo Hara Pyaz

Potatoes, peeled, cut into cubes	400 g/2 cups
Oil	20 ml/1 tbsp
Mustard seeds	3 g/½ tsp
Red chilis, dried	4
Curry leaves	one sprig
Turmeric–	10 g/2 tsp
Chili powder	5 g/1 tsp
Tomatoes, chopped	50 g/¼ cup
Scallions, chopped	100 g/½ cup
Salt	to taste
Chaat masala (see page 49)–	5 g/1 tsp
Coriander leaves, chopped	5 g/1 tsp

Boil the potatoes with some salt and half the turmeric until they are cooked through. This should take about twenty minutes. Drain the water and spread the potatoes on a tray to cool.

Heat the oil in a heavy-bottomed pan. Add the mustard, chilis, and curry leaves. When the seeds crackle, add the potatoes and cook them on high heat until they are golden and crisp on the surface. Sprinkle with turmeric, chili powder, some salt, and add the tomatoes. Reduce the heat to a simmer. Add the scallions and stir gently until the tomatoes are pulpy. Sprinkle in the chaat masala, stir, and taste. Adjust the seasoning, if required. Stir in the chopped coriander leaves. Serve hot.

Potato Vindaloo

Vindaloo is probably the most well known, and most maligned sauce found on Indian restaurant menus. While Goans, who invented the dish, created a well balanced ratio of spicy, hot, and sour flavors, the "overseas" version has caused one to expect an extremely hot and spicy curry.

'Aloo' at the end of the name of the dish would seem to suggest that a vindaloo should contain potatoes. In fact, vindaloo never contained potatoes. The main ingredient was pork. The word is actually not Indian, but an amalgam of two

Portuguese words, 'vinho,' which means wine and denotes the use of wine vinegar, and 'alho,' which means garlic.

Potatoes, peeled and cut into quarters	400 g/2 cups
Oil	20 ml/1 tbsp
Onions, chopped	70 g/⅓ cup
Garlic, chopped	20 g/1 tbsp
Ginger, peeled	5 g/1 tsp
Red chillies, dried	6
Cumin seeds	a pinch
Coriander seeds	a pinch
Cinnamon stick	1 piece, about 2–3 inches in length
Green cardamon	6 pods
Cloves	4 buds
Turmeric	5 g/1 tsp
Malt vinegar	50 ml/¼ cup
Fresh chilis, slit (see page 29)	2
Sugar	5 g/1 tsp
Salt	to taste

In a food processor, process the ginger, red chilis, cumin, coriander seeds, cinnamon, cardamom, cloves, and turmeric with the malt vinegar to obtain a smooth paste. Heat the oil in a heavy pan and fry the onions until they are soft and golden. Add the garlic and stir until it changes color. Add the spice paste and stir over medium heat until the oils separate from the paste. Add 500 ml (2½ cups) of water, the potatoes, slit green chillies, and salt. Simmer until the potatoes are cooked through. Add the sugar and taste. Adjust the seasoning, if required. This curry should have a sauce of a thick, coating consistency. Its thickness can be modified by adding water or by simmering to thicken, as necessary. Just before serving bring the sauce to a boil. Serve hot.

Potatoes and Cauliflower Tossed with Bengali Five Spice

Aloo Gobir Chorchorri

Panch Phoran, also known as the Bengali five spices, is likely the most often used combination of spices used in cooking in the east of India in those areas that span the states of Bengal, Orissa, Assam, Meghalaya, Nagaland, and parts of Bihar. See the recipe below.

Potatoes, peeled and diced	150 g/¾ cup
Cauliflower, cut into tiny florets	250 g/1 ¼ cup
Mustard oil	20 ml/1 tbsp
Panch phoran	5 g/1 tsp
Red chili powder	10 g/2 tsp
Turmeric	10 g/2 tsp
Salt	to taste

Heat the oil in a heavy-bottomed pan until it just smokes. Remove from the heat and add the panch phoran. When the seeds splutter, return the pan to the stove and add the potatoes, cauliflower, salt, and turmeric. Reduce the heat and sprinkle in a bit of water to prevent the spices from burning. Stir often until the vegetables are soft. Add the chili powder, cover tightly, and simmer until the vegetables are done. If you have trouble about the vegetables cooking through, add a couple of teaspoons of water and cook, covered tightly, for an additional five minutes. Taste and adjust the seasoning if required. Serve hot.

Bengali Five Spice/Panch Phoran

Although the blend is quite simple to prepare and will keep well for a couple of months in airtight containers, it is available readymade in most Indian provision stores.

Since you may not require more than 5g/1 tsp at a time, it is better to prepare only a small quantity for storage.

The mix is equal quantities of mustard seeds, fenugreek seeds, black onion seeds, fennel seeds, and cumin seeds. They are not ground, but merely mixed and stored. A teaspoon of each spice will keep you ready for a number of dishes into the future.

Tip: Cut the vegetables into small pieces which helps them cook faster and in a minimal amount of liquid thus keeping this a rather 'dry' dish, the flavor of which is not diluted by water.

Potatoes Cooked In Bengali Five Spice
Aloo Chorchorri

Potatoes, peeled and quartered	300 g/1 ½ cup
Panch phoran (see page 36)	5 g/1 tsp
Mustard oil	40 ml/2 tbsp
Turmeric	5 g/1 tsp
Fresh chilis	4
Salt	to taste

Heat the oil in a heavy-bottomed pan. When it smokes, add the panch phoran. When the seeds crackle, add the potatoes and some salt. Stir the potatoes over low heat until they change from white to straw or a pale gold color. Add the fresh chilis, turmeric, and 80 ml/3/8 cup of water and continue simmering until the potatoes are done and most of the liquid has been absorbed. Add water during cooking if this should be necessary. Check seasoning and remove from heat. Serve hot.

Potatoes in Poppy-Seed Gravy
Aloo Posto Chorchorri

This is one of my favorite potato dishes. It is simple and tasty. I am a potato person. I love the strong earthy flavors that this dish exhudes. This is a classic example of the magic of panch phoran, the Bengali five-spice mix, with poppy seeds. This dish is traditionally served with luchi, a Bengali fried bread.

Potatoes, peeled and quartered	300 g/1 ½ cup
Poppy seeds	40 g/2 tbsp
Panch phoran (see page 36)	5 g/1 tsp
Mustard oil	40 ml/2 tbsp
Turmeric	5 g/1 tsp

Fresh chilis, slit (see page 29)	4
Salt	to taste

Soak the poppy seeds in 50 ml (¼ cup) of hot water for half an hour, then process them to a fine paste in a food processor.

Heat the oil in a heavy-bottomed pot. When it smokes, add the panch phoran. When it crackles, add the potatoes and fry until they turn golden. Add the turmeric and the slit green chilis and some salt. Add the poppy seed paste and fry until the mixture thickens. Stir constantly to prevent burning. Add 50 ml/¼ cup of water. Cover and simmer for about ten minutes to allow the potatoes to cook through. Check and adjust seasoning, if required. Remove from heat. Serve hot.

Tip: The difference between puri/poori and luchi is the flour. Luchi uses refined flour; puri, wholewheat.

Potatoes In Tangy Spiced Gravy
Aloo Dum

Potatoes, peeled, diced, and boiled	500 g/1.1 lb
Onions, chopped	150 g/¾ cup
Garlic, chopped	10 g/2 tsp
Tamarind pulp/paste	20 g/1 tbsp
Chili powder	10 g/2 tsp
Turmeric	10 g/2 tsp
Sugar	20 g/1 tbsp
Cinnamon stick	1 piece, about 2–3 inches in length
Green cardamom	3 pods
Cloves	3 g/½ tsp
Bay leaf	2
Oil	40 ml/2 tbsp
Ghee/clarified butter	20 g/1 tbsp
Water	400 ml/2 cups
Salt	to taste

In a heavy-bottomed pan, heat the oil and clarified butter. Add the whole spices—cinnamon, cardamom, cloves, and bay leaves. Stir on high heat for a brief period to roast the spices. Reduce the heat and add the onions. Cook until golden brown. Add the garlic. When garlic has softened, add the chili, turmeric, and potatoes. Reduce the heat to low for a few more minutes and stir continuously to prevent the spices from sticking. Sprinkle in some salt. Add the tamarind pulp, water, and sugar. Bring the sauce to a boil. Reduce the heat to simmer and stir occasionally until the sauce thickens, coating the potatoes. Check taste and remove from heat. You may wish to remove the cinnamon stick and bay leaf before serving though this conveys the authenticity of the ingredients used.

Stewed Potatoes and Beans in Lightly Spiced Coconut Milk

Kizhanga Ishtew

Potatoes, peeled and cut into 1-inch cubes	400 g/2 cups
French beans/string beans cut into 1-inch pieces	100 g/½ cup
Coconut oil	30 ml/1 ½ tbsp
Black peppercorns	5 g/1 tsp
Cinnamon sticks	2 pieces, about 2–3 inches in length
Green cardamom	5 pods
Cloves	5 buds
Ginger, fresh, chopped	20 g/1 tbsp
Fresh chilies, chopped	15 g/3 tsp
Coconut milk	450 ml/2 ¼ cup
Salt	to taste
Coriander leaves, chopped	10 g/2 tsp

Heat the oil in a thick-bottomed pot. Add the peppercorns, cinnamon, cardamom, and cloves. When the spices begin to swell and change color add the potatoes and stir them on medium heat for about five minutes.

Add the ginger and chilies, continuing to stir for another five minutes.

Add 500 ml/2½ cups of water and simmer for fifteen minutes until the potatoes are cooked half way through.

Add the coconut milk and bring the sauce to a rapid boil for two minutes.

Then add the beans and salt. Reduce the heat to simmer and cook for ten minutes or until the sauce thickens to the consistency of a thick soup.

Taste and adjust the seasonings, if necessary. Stir in the fresh coriander and serve hot.

Potatoes Cooked with Fenugreek Leaves

Aloo Methi

A memory I will always cherish is owning my very own organic farm. My recall always finds me in my overalls digging potatoes in the garden. I remember the wonderful bloom of the mustard flowers, the fragrance of freshly crushed fennel seeds in my hands, and the tenderness and sweetness of fenugreek leaves.

I often served this classic potato recipe during that time. I am sure that you will enjoy the dish equally as well using store-bought produce.

Potatoes, peeled, quartered, and boiled	400 g/2 cups
Oil	20 ml/1 tbsp
Cumin seeds	5 g/1 tsp
Onions, chopped	50 g/¼ cup
Garlic, chopped	5 g/1 tsp
Ginger, chopped	5 g/1 tsp
Fresh chilis, chopped	10 g/2 tsp
Fenugreek leaves, chopped	70 g/⅓ cup
Salt	to taste
Lemon	1
Coriander leaves, chopped	5 g/1 tsp

Heat the oil in a heavy-bottomed pan and add the cumin seeds. When they crackle, add the onions and stir gently until they soften and turn golden. Add the chopped garlic. When that softens, increase the heat and add the potatoes. Stir the potatoes occasionally until they are seared and brown. Add the fresh chilis, ginger, and salt. Toss all the ingredients together a few times, stirring in the fenugreek leaves. When the leaves wilt, remove the pan from the heat, sprinkle on the lemon juice and chopped coriander leaves. Taste, adjust seasoning, if necessary, and serve hot.

Maharashtrian Spice-Tossed Potatoes
Battanteche Sukhe

Potatoes, peeled, diced and boiled	400 g/2 cups
Oil	20 ml/1 tbsp
Cumin seeds	3 g/½ tsp
Red chilis, dried	2
Turmeric	5 g/1 tsp
Ginger, shredded	5 g/1 tsp
Fresh chilis, chopped	5 g/1 tsp
Coriander seeds	5 g/1 tsp
Juice of one lemon	
Coriander leaves, chopped	5 g/1 tsp

Roast the coriander seeds in a dry pan. Allow them to cool and gently crush them in the palm of your hand or use a mortar and pestle.

Heat the oil in a heavy-bottomed pan and add the crushed cumin seeds. When the seeds crackle, add the red chilis and potatoes and cook, turning them occasionally to ensure that they become evenly golden and crusted. Add the salt, turmeric, ginger, and fresh chilis. Toss gently, sprinkle in the coriander seeds and lemon juice and remove from the heat. Taste and adjust the seasoning, if necessary. Stir in the coriander leaves and serve hot.

Calcutta-Style Potato Curry
Aloo jhol

The secrets in this recipe along with some others scattered throughout this book were revealed to me by a singularly remarkable woman. Mrs. Purnima Bhattacharya is, in my humble opinion, the guardian of the holy grail of Bengali culinary tradition.

Potatoes, peeled and cut into quarters	500 g/1 lb
Oil	50 ml/¼ cup
Cumin seeds	10 g/2 tsp
Bay leaf	1
Ginger, peeled	10 g/1 tsp
Garlic, peeled	20 g/1 tbsp
Fresh chilis, chopped	10 g/2 tsp
Turmeric	10 g/2 tsp
Chili powder	5 g/1 tsp
Coriander, ground	5 g/1 tsp
Tomatoes, cut into quarters	100 g/1 cup
Salt	to taste
Coriander leaves, chopped	10 g/2 tsp

Process the ginger, garlic and green chilis together to a coarse paste.

Heat the oil and fry the potatoes on moderate heat until they are golden brown. Remove from the oil with a slotted spoon and keep aside for later use.

Reheat the oil in which the potatoes were fried. Sprinkle in the cumin seeds and add the bay leaf. When the cumin crackles add the processed paste and stir over gentle heat to prevent it from sticking to the bottom and burning. Add the ground spices, stir and pour in 450 ml (2 ¼ cups) of water. Check the seasoning and add the potatoes. Simmer until the potatoes are done. Add the tomatoes and bring to a boil. Check the seasonings again, simmer until the sauce thickens moderately and remove from the heat. Sprinkle in the coriander leaves and serve hot.

Spinach

Popeye will tell you that spinach is the greatest vegetable ever discovered, and I say that you should listen to the sailor man. Spinach has a long association with human well-being.

This flowering plant, farmed for its tender, succulent leaves, became known for its high iron content. However, it is not as high as was originally thought because there was an error in the calculation of the values due to a misplaced decimal. This error which was found in the 1930s claimed an iron content ten times higher than it actually is. It is in any case also a great source of Vitamins A, C and E, folic acid and several antioxidants vital to human nutrition.

Fresh spinach leaves begin to lose their nutritional value after being stored for a few days. Refrigeration slows this process down while freezing or canning spinach preserves much of its original nutrition.

Spinach was first found in Persia more than two thousand years ago and it moved from there to Rome and Greece where it was first cultivated. Several conquests later it appeared all over the world. Europeans were the last to embrace spinach—it finally appeared there in the 14th century. Its impact was tremendous and it has remained important to this day.

Potatoes in a Mildly Spiced Spinach Gravy
Aloo Palak

Potatoes, peeled and cut into 1-inch cubes	250 g/1 ¼ cups
Spinach leaves, rinsed	1 kg/2 lbs
Oil	20 ml/1 tbsp
Garlic, chopped	10 g/2 tsp
Dried red chilis, whole	3
Cumin seeds	5 g/1 tsp
Chili powder	5 g/1 tsp

Green cardamom	5 pods
Salt	to taste

Add the spinach to boiling water. Stir a few times, just long enough to become bright green and somewhat tender. Remove and shock them in cold running water to retain the color. Drain well and process them to a smooth paste in a food processor.

Put the potatoes into boiling salted water, removing them as soon as the water comes to a boil again. Spread them on a tray to cool and dry out a bit.

Heat the oil in a heavy-bottomed pot and add the garlic, chilis, and cumin. Stir over low heat until the garlic begins to soften. Add the potatoes and stir them gently until they begin to brown, add the spinach mixture, chili powder, cardamom pods, and salt. Simmer on low heat. Stir frequently to prevent the mixture from sticking to the bottom of the pot. If required, thin the sauce with a bit of water. Taste and adjust the seasonings if required. When the potatoes are cooked through and the sauce is smooth and thick, remove from the heat and serve hot.

Note: Palak paneer is prepared in the same way by substituting paneer for the potatoes.

Stir-Fried Spinach and Fenugreek Leaves
Ghota Hua Palak aur Methi Ka Saag

Fenugreek leaves, rinsed/methi patta	100 g/½ cup (after cooking)
Spinach, rinsed	250 g/1¼ cups (after cooking)
Dry red chili	1
Cashew nut paste	20 g/1 tbsp
Ginger paste	5 g/1 tsp
Chopped garlic	10 g/2 tsp
Chopped onions	20 g/1 tbsp
Chopped tomatoes	30 g/1½ tbsp
Chopped fresh chili –	1
Cumin seeds	a pinch
Turmeric powder	a pinch

Chilli powder	a pinch
Cream	10 ml/2 tsp
Garam masala powder	a pinch
Ghee	5 g/1 tsp
Chopped coriander leaves	5 g/1 tsp
Salt	to taste
Chaat masala	a pinch

In boiling salted water, blanch the spinach and fenugreek leaves separately. Remove and run them under cool water, squeezing out the excess water. Roughly chop the leaves and keep aside.

In a heavy-bottom pot, heat the oil and add the cumin seeds and the dried red chili. When the seeds crackle, add the chopped onions and cook until they are golden. Add in the garlic and ginger paste, stir until the garlic changes color. Add the spinach, fenugreek, fresh chili, turmeric, chili powder, salt, and cashew nut paste. Stir to mix well. If the leaves begin to burn, sprinkle in a little water. After cooking for a couple of minutes, add in the cream and reduce the heat to simmer. Add the tomatoes and simmer until the tomatoes are pulpy. Check and adjust seasoning. Add the ghee and sprinkle on the chaat masala. Stir and serve hot.

Spinach Leaves with Ginger and Tomatoes

Adraki Palak

Spinach leaves, rinsed	800 g/4 cups (pressed tight)
Oil	20 ml/1 tbsp
Mustard seeds	a pinch
Cumin seeds	a pinch
Chopped ginger	15 g/3 tsp
Chopped fresh chillies	10 g/2 tsp
Chopped tomatoes	100 g/½ cup
Salt	to taste
Coriander seeds, roasted and lightly crushed	10 g/2 tsp
Juice of one lemon	

Heat the oil in a heavy-bottom pot and add the mustard and cumin seeds. When they crackle, add the ginger and chillies and stir on low heat until they soften. Add the tomatoes and simmer unti they turn pulpy. Stir in the spinach leaves and salt and simmer until the spinach is soft. Sprinkle in the coriander seeds and lemon juice. Stir to mix well, taste, and adjust the seasonings, if required. Serve hot.

Spinach Leaves Tossed with Mustard
Sarson Palak

Spinach leaves	800 g/4 cups (pressed tight)
Mustard seeds	15 g/3 tsp
Green chilies	2
Turmeric powder	a pinch
Mustard oil	10 ml/2 tsp
Ginger, grated	5 g/1 tsp
Salt	to taste

Place the mustard seeds in a small bowl, cover them with hot water and set aside for twenty minutes. Grind the seeds to a coarse paste with the green chilies and turmeric in a food processor, or pound them with a mortar and pestle.

Heat the oil in a pan until it smokes. Reduce the heat and add the mustard paste. Stir continuously on medium heat for about three minutes. Add the spinach leaves and salt, stirring until the leaves wilt. Taste and adjust the seasoning, if required, and serve hot.

Pumpkin

Botanic and culinary experts have long been at loggerheads over this vegetable that is so loved the world over. Technically a fruit, in culinary terms it is treated as a vegetable.

The first pumpkins came from Central America. Its modern name was anglicised from the Greek word "Pepon" which means large melon and is the reason why pumpkin seeds are called pepitas.

Bengalis especially adore the pumpkin. It is said that they use every part of the plant but the stem: The fruit, the flowers, the tender green leaves, the young shoots, and even young roots may be eaten.

Pumpkin is often used in comfort foods and, in ancient days, as an ingredient in aphrodisiacal recipes. It is known to be healthful as well since about 90% of it is water and is a great source of Vitamin A and potassium. Roasted pumpkin seeds are a source of iron, zinc, potassium, and magnesium, and are very tasty.

There are two varieties of pumpkin: the orange, sweeter version, and a milder, white version. Both are squashes. However, I'm told that Americans don't think of pumpkins as a squash.

In India we have the red variety of squash that we call red pumpkin. In America that same variety, the Halloween pumpkin, is referred to as simply "pumpkin." There are varieties of squash that are smaller in size and differently colored called squash in both India and America. You have pattypan squash, acorn squash, spaghetti squash. Zucchini is a type of squash and so is what you call "yellow squash," which is actually a yellow zucchini.

In India we have differently shaped and colored squashes and gourds like ash gourd, snake gourd, sponge gourd, and ridge gourd which are vegetables normally seen only in this part of the world. Sponge gourd is probably familiar to you by the name loofah. In its immature state it is delicious, but grown up and dried it is used in the shower as an exfoliant.

Pumpkin, squash, and gourd are essentially the same things. They are referred to differently in different cultures. To Americans, pumpkins are pumpkins, squash is other than pumpkin and is eaten, while gourd is squash that could be eaten but is instead dried, sometimes shellaced, and used decoratively.

For recipes that call for pumpkin, any type of the red version is suitable. For recipes that use the white version, it could be substituted by zucchini or even sweet potato. Sweet potato is, of course, vastly different, but it absorbs flavors well when used as a substitute and can enhance a dish significantly.

With a bow to the electronically interactive nature of this book, if any of my readers refer to pumpkins or squashes in a different manner please let me hear from you at zubin@chefzubin.com

White Pumpkin Simmered with Spices and Coconut Milk
Lauki Kanchoo

White pumpkin, seeded, peeled, and diced	400 g/2 cups
Oil	20 ml/1 tbsp
Mustard seeds	a pinch
Curry leaves	1 sprig
Sliced onions	50 g/¼ cup
Turmeric	10 g/2 tsp
Fresh chilis, slit (see page 29)	2
Coconut milk	150 ml/¾ cup
Grated coconut	70 g/⅓ cup
Sugar	a pinch
Salt	to taste
Coriander leaves, chopped	5 g/1 tsp

Heat the oil in a heavy-bottomed pan and add the mustard seeds. When they crackle, add the curry leaves and sliced onions. Gently stir until the onions are golden. Add the pumpkin, turmeric, slit fresh chilis, and salt. Continue to stir over low heat for about five minutes. Pour in the coconut milk and simmer for about ten minutes. Taste and adjust the seasoning, if required. When the pumpkin is almost done, stir in the grated coconut and sugar. When the liquid thoroughly coats the pumpkin, stir in the coriander leaves and serve hot.

Spiced Pumpkin
Masala Kadoo

Red pumpkin, peeled, seeded, and cut into 1-inch cubes	400 g/2 cups
Oil	20 ml/1 tbsp
Fennel seeds	a pinch
Mustard seeds	a pinch
Onions, sliced	50 g/¼ cup
Garlic, chopped	5 g/1 tsp
Ginger, shredded	5 g/1 tsp
Fresh chilis, chopped	10 g/2 tsp
Turmeric	10 g/2 tsp
Salt	to taste
Sugar	5 g/1 tsp
Coriander leaves, chopped	5 g/1 tsp

Heat the oil in a heavy-bottomed pan. Add fennel and mustard seeds. When they crackle, add the onions and cook them gently until they are golden. Add fresh chilis, shredded ginger, turmeric, salt, and the pumpkin. Stir on low heat until the pumpkin begins to become tender. Sprinkle in a few drops of water to prevent the spices from burning. (As pumpkin is high in sugar, it tends to caramelize. Sprinkling a bit of water prevents this.) When the pumpkin is cooked through and soft, add the sugar. Taste and adjust the seasoning if required. Stir in the coriander leaves and serve hot.

Tangy South Indian Pumpkin Curry
Parangi Kai Puli Curry

Although the red pumpkin is commonly used throughout the world, in India it is turned into a variety of tantalizing and appetizing dishes. Many cultures in the world shun this vegetable, declaring it sustenance for the "poor." I am sure that the smallest taste of this beautiful curry will convince them otherwise.

Pumpkin peeled, seeded, and cut into cubes	400 g/2 cups
Oil	20 ml/1 tbsp

Shallots, chopped	50 g/¼ cup
Garlic, chopped	20 g/1 tbsp
Coriander seeds	5 g/1 tsp
Dried chilis	4
Chili powder	5 g/1 tsp
Turmeric	10 g/2 tsp
Tamarind pulp	10 g/2 tsp
Tomatoes, cut into quarters	70 g/⅓ cup
Palm sugar or cane sugar	20 g/1 tbsp
Fennel seeds	5 g/1 tsp
Salt	to taste

Heat the oil in a heavy-bottomed pot and add the shallots. Stir over medium heat until they are soft. Add garlic, coriander seeds, and dried chilis. When the garlic softens and begins to change color, add the pumpkin and continue to stir until the outer portions of the cubes of pumpkin begin to appear soft and translucent. Add the chili powder, turmeric, salt, tamarind pulp, tomatoes, and 500 ml / 2½ cups of water and reduce the heat. Simmer covered for about ten minutes until the pumpkin is cooked about halfway through. Add the fennel seeds and the sugar and continue to simmer until the gravy thickens and the pumpkin cubes soften, but remain whole. Taste and adjust the seasonings, if necessary. The gravy can be thinned by adding water and bringing it again to a boil. Serve hot.

Slow Braised Pumpkin with Sesame Seeds

Tilwale Kaddu

Growing up in Bombay (now Mumbai) brought me together with an odd group of characters. To this day I have never figured out how my old neighborhood attracted the people it did—from beggars and thieves to office executives and wannabe models. Although the neighborhood had its share of seedy characters, it was quite safe, in fact protected by the same unsavory characters who inhabited it.

Caitan was the local drunk and resident beggar. He was scruffy and short, with a balding head that would have made a Franciscan Friar proud. Whenever he managed to squeeze some coins from someone, he flew straight to the local tipple shop and had his fill. He would soon step out into the noonday sun, blind drunk and scream at the top of his lungs, "Caitan is king!"

Doing this earned him the amused affection of the residents. We kids sometimes sneaked off to his little hut on the top of the hill with vegetables we had pilfered from the family's weekly shopping. On one such visit I arrived with a pumpkin and was invited to stay for supper. In that tiny hovel, where most of the furniture was littered with empty bottles, Caitan managed to transform that pumpkin into something heavenly. Whenever I again asked him to make this dish for me I had to be sure that he was absolutely drunk. He never remembered the recipe when he was sober.

Pumpkin, peeled, and cut into 1-inch cubes	500 g/1 lb
Sesame seeds, roasted	50 g/¼ cup
Mustard oil	20 ml/1 tbsp
Mustard seeds	5 g/1 tsp
Coriander seeds	3 g/½ tsp
Dried chilis	4
Turmeric	10 g/2 tsp
Sugar	5 g/1 tsp
Salt	to taste
Coriander leaves, chopped	5 g/1 tsp

Heat the oil until it begins to smoke. Let it cool a bit and add the mustard seeds, coriander seeds, and dried red chilis. When the seeds crackle, add the pumpkin and stir together over high heat for about five minutes. Reduce the heat, add the salt and turmeric, cover, and simmer for about ten minutes until the pumpkin is almost cooked. In another pan, gently toast the sesame seeds; add them with the sugar to the pumpkin. Keep stirring and simmering for ten minutes until the pumpkin is tender. Taste and adjust the seasoning if required, stir in the coriander leaves and serve hot.

Stewed Pumpkin

Kumro Dalna

Cinnamon sticks	2 pieces, about 2–3 inches in length
Cloves	4 buds

Green cardamom	3 pods
Ginger, peeled and chopped	10 g/2 tsp
Mustard oil	20 ml/1 tbsp
Potatoes, peeled and diced	150 g/¾ cup
Bay leaf	2
Cumin seeds	3 g/½ tsp
Dried red chili	2
Tomato, chopped	50 g/¼ cup
Turmeric	5 g/1 tsp
Coriander powder	3 g/½ tsp
Chili powder	5 g/1 tsp
Pumpkin, peeled and cut into 1-inch cubes	400 g/2 cups
Sugar	5 g/1 tsp
Salt	to taste

Grind the cinnamon, cloves, cardamom, and ginger to a paste. Reserve for later use. Heat up the mustard oil and fry the potatoes until golden. Remove and keep aside to drain on an absorbent kitchen towel.

Reheat the same oil and add the bay leaf, the cumin seeds, and the chili. When the cumin seeds crackle, add the ginger-spice paste. Fry the mixture on low heat, then add the turmeric, coriander, and chili powder. Add the diced pumpkin and stir a bit. Add the chopped tomatoes and continue simmering.

When the pumpkin has softened put in the fried potatoes, salt, and sugar. Reheat for the potato, adjust the seasoning, if necessary, and serve hot.

White Pumpkin and Coconut
Lau Ghonto

Bori, sun-dried lentil dumplings are available readymade at many Indian provision shops. They are also known as masala vade and punjabi vadiyan, a close substitute. They are made by dropping dollops of soaked and finely ground lentils onto sheets and are then left in the sun to dry.

White pumpkin, diced	500 g/1.1 lb
Mustard oil	40 ml/2 tbsp

Mustard seeds	5 g/1 tsp
Dried red chilis	6
Turmeric	5 g/1 tsp
Sugar	10 g/2 tsp
Milk	50 ml/¼ cup
Whole wheat flour	20 g/1 tbsp
Coconut, grated	20 g/1 tbsp
Bori/Sundried lentil dumplings (optional)	40 g/2 tbsp

Heat the oil in a heavy-bottomed pan and add the mustard seeds. When they splutter add the dried chilis and the pumpkin. Add salt and turmeric. Reduce the heat to a simmer and stir occasionally.

Fry the bori, cool, grind them coarse, and reserve. Whisk together the milk and whole-wheat flour to make a slurry.

When the pumpkin is almost cooked through, increase the heat to a boil and add the sugar and the slurry, which acts as a thickening agent, and will begin to thicken the pumpkin almost immediately. Stir a bit and add the grated coconut. Taste and adjust seasoning if required, sprinkle with ground bori and when the sauce coats the pumpkin, remove and serve hot.

White Pumpkin and Coconut Stew

Lau Shukto

White pumpkin, diced	500 g/1.1 lb
Mustard seeds	a pinch
Fenugreek seeds	a pinch
Mustard seeds, soaked in water and ground to a paste	5 g/1 tsp
Poppy seeds, soaked in water and ground to a paste	5 g/1 tsp
Turmeric	5 g/1 tsp
Coconut, grated	10 g/2 tsp
Milk	100 ml/½ cup
Sugar	5 g/1 tsp
Salt	to taste

Ginger, chopped	5 g/1 tsp
Mustard oil	20 ml/1 tbsp

In a heavy-bottomed pan, heat the mustard oil until it smokes. Add the mustard and fenugreek seeds. When they crackle, add the chopped ginger and the diced white pumpkin. Stir, add some salt, cover, and simmer for about five minutes until the pumpkin is about half done. Add the poppy and mustard pastes and the coconut. Stir a bit, adding a little water, if necessary. Add the milk and sugar and cook to reduce, until the gravy is thick. Serve hot with rice.

White Pumpkin Relish
Kumbalanga Pachadi

Coconut oil	10 ml/2 tsp
Mustard seeds	a pinch
Fenugreek seeds	a pinch
Asafoetida powder	a pinch
Fresh chilis, slit (see page 29)	5
Curry leaves	2 sprigs
Yogurt, beaten	200 g/1 cup
Sugar	10 g/2 tsp
Salt	to taste
White pumpkin, cut into 1-inch cubes and boiled until soft	100 g/½ cup

In a pan, heat the coconut oil. Add the mustard and fenugreek seeds. When the seeds crackle, add the asafoetida and stir for a couple of minutes, add the fresh chilis and fry them until they turn bright green. Add the curry leaves and the beaten yogurt with the salt, sugar and white pumpkin cubes. Stir gently on high heat for a minute. Taste and adjust seasoning, if necessary, and serve warm as a side dish or as accompaniment to a main course.

Spiced Braised Pumpkin

Hara Kaddu Masala

Tender young green pumpkins are available all over India during the summer months and are wonderful prepared in this manner. You may be able to find them in the U.S. in season. This recipe is dependent on green pumpkin availability during the summer months and people tend to make it often, before the vegetable begins to ripen by early autumn.

Zucchini or yellow squash may be used as a substitute.

Pumpkin, young, tender	600 g/3 cups
Oil	20 ml/1 tbsp
Mustard seeds	a pinch
Curry leaves	one sprig
Red chilis, dried	2
Onions, sliced	100 g/½ cup
Fresh chilis, chopped	5 g/1 tsp
Ginger, shredded	5 g/1 tsp
Coriander seeds, roasted	a pinch
Coconut, grated	20 g/1 tbsp
Salt	to taste
Sugar	a pinch
Dried mango powder/amchur	a pinch
Coriander leaves, chopped	5 g/1 tsp

Grate the skin and flesh of the pumpkin. You can cut the pumpkin into manageable pieces. Scoop out the inner pith and seeds with a spoon or a melon baller and discard. Rub the pieces on a grater and collect the shredded flesh.

Heat the oil in a heavy-bottomed pot and add the mustard seeds, curry leaves, and dried red chilis. When the seeds splutter, add the sliced onions and stir them on low heat until they are soft and transparent. Add the grated pumpkin, fresh chilis, and ginger, continuing to stir for about five minutes until the pumpkin softens. Crush the coriander seeds in a mortar with a pestle. Sprinkle this over the pumpkin along with the coconut, salt, sugar, amchur, and the coriander leaves. Taste and adjust the seasoning if required. Stir for a few minutes until the liquid is absorbed and the pumpkin is tender. Serve hot.

Pumpkin Dumplings Simmered in Tangy Nut Gravy
Kaddu ke Koftey

Pumpkin, peeled and cut into 1-inch cubes	400 g/2 cups
Chickpea flour	50 g/½ cup
Oil	20 ml/1 tbsp
Cinnamon sticks	2 pieces, about 2–3 inches in length
Green cardamom	4 pods
Cloves	6 buds
Onions, chopped	150 g/¾ cup
Fresh chilis	10 g/2 tsp
Garlic, chopped	10 g/2 tsp
Ginger, shredded	10 g/2 tsp
Tamarind pulp	20 ml/1 tbsp
Cashew nuts, crushed	40 g/2 tbsp
Salt	to taste
Coriander leaves, chopped	5 g/1 tsp

Boil the pumpkin in salted water until it is soft. Remove from the pot with a slotted spoon. Mash and squeeze the pumpkin in cheesecloth to remove the excess liquid and place in large bowl.

Gently roast the chickpea flour in a dry pan until it turns golden. Mix this into the mashed pumpkin and knead them together to form a soft dough. Form into golf ball-sized balls and drop them into a pot of boiling, salted water. When they rise to the surface allow them to simmer for five minutes in order that they cook through. Remove with a slotted spoon and set aside to cool.

Heat the oil in a heavy-bottomed pot. Add the cinnamon, cardamom and cloves. When the cardomom begins to swell, add the chopped onions and stir until golden. Add the chilis, garlic, and ginger and stir occasionally until the garlic begins to color. Add the tamarind pulp, a bit of salt and 200 ml/a cup of water. Reduce the heat to a gentle simmer. Taste and adjust the seasoning of the sauce, if required. Add the dumplings to the pot along with the nuts. Simmer until hot, then bring the liquid to a boil for a minute. Finish off with coriander leaves and serve hot.

Eggplant

I love shiny, smooth-skinned, purple eggplants. They are absolutely heavenly to prepare and always impress.

Botanically speaking, the eggplant is a fruit. I can't think of a vegetable or fruit with a greater number of globally recognized names and pseudonyms. Eggplant, aubergine, brinjal, melanzana and baingan are some I can think of. In India, where it may have originated, one of its names, brinjal, is said to have originated in the south where it suggests the title, "King of the vegetables."

Because it is a member of the nightshade family (Solanaceae), it was not at that time well received—it was viewed with suspicion as poisonous, which, obviously, it is not

Baby Eggplant Cooked in Peanut-Thickened Gravy

Baingan aur Moongphali ka Milan

Baby eggplants (see below for preparation)	250 g/1¼ cup
Salt	to taste
Poppy seeds	10 g/2 tsp
White sesame seeds	10 g/2 tsp
Mustard seeds	5 g/2 tsp
Fresh chilis	10 g/2 tsp
Oil	20 ml/1 tbsp
Onions, chopped	50 g/¼ cup
Garlic, chopped	5 g/1 tsp
Tomatoes, chopped	100 g/½ cup
Chili powder	5 g/1 tsp
Turmeric–	10 g/2 tsp

Peanuts, roasted	50 g/¼ cup
Sugar	10 g/2 tsp
Coriander leaves, chopped	10 g/2 tsp

Wash the eggplants well and pat them dry. Leave the stems on and cut them from the base upward into quarters up to three-fourths of the way. This way the eggplant holds together while cooking. Rub the insides well with half the turmeric and a bit of salt and keep them in a cool place for half an hour. This ensures that the salt flavor penetrates the eggplant resulting in a tastier dish.

Soak the poppy, sesame, and mustard seeds in warm water for fifteen minutes, drain, and grind them along with the fresh chilis to a smooth paste. Coat the insides of the eggplants with paste and place them in a moderately hot oven (160°C/325°F) for ten minutes until they are evenly golden. Remove from the heat and allow to cool.

Heat the oil and sauté the onions until they are golden. Add the garlic. When the garlic begins to change color, add the tomatoes, salt, chili powder, and turmeric. Simmer until the tomatoes are pulpy. Add ½ cup of water and the eggplant and simmer for about ten minutes. Lightly crush the peanuts and sprinkle them in along with the sugar. When the sauce thickens and coats the eggplant, taste and adjust the seasoning, if required Stir in the coriander leaves and serve hot. The stems are discarded after the meal.

Tip: If baby eggplants are unavailable, cut larger eggplant into 1-inch cubes and prepare in the same manner. You can splash on a dash of tamarind or ginger to give it some added zing.

Spiced Eggplant Hash

Baingan Bharta

Although many people do not seize upon this style of eggplant preparation because of its pasty texture, the flavor of this dish is absolutely irresistible. The roasted, smoky taste and the nuttiness it gets from the onion seeds create an addicting dish and a palate sensation on which all can agree. It regularly appears on U.S. restaurant menus.

| Eggplant (see below for preparation) | 400 g/2 cups |
| Oil | 20 ml/1 tbsp |

Cumin seeds	a pinch
Nigella/kalonji	a pinch
Ginger, shredded	a pinch
Garlic, chopped	5 g/1 tsp
Tomatoes, chopped	75 g/⅓ cup
Turmeric	5 g/1 tsp
Chili powder	5 g/1 tsp
Fresh chilis, slit (see page 29)	2
Salt	to taste
Coriander leaves, chopped	5 g/1 tsp
Juice of one lemon	

Roast the eggplant over an open flame until the skin has been evenly charred black. Alternatively, the eggplant can be placed in a hot oven (190°C/375°F) for about fifteen minutes to achieve the same results.

Peel and discard the skin and seeds and coarsely chop up the flesh.

Heat the oil in a heavy-bottomed pan. Add the cumin seeds and nigella. When they crackle, add the ginger and garlic, stirring until they turn soft. Add the tomatoes and stir on high heat for two minutes. Add the chopped eggplant, turmeric, chili powder, slit fresh chilis, and salt. Simmer for about ten minutes until the eggplant is soft and pulpy, as though it had been mashed. Taste and adjust the seasoning, if required. Stir in the coriander leaves, sprinkle on the lemon juice, and serve hot.

Eggplant Simmered in Tamarind Gravy
Beguner Tak

Baby eggplant	500 g/1 lb
Oil	for deep-frying, heated to 190°C/375°F
Salt	to taste
Turmeric	20 g/1 tbsp
Chili powder	10 g/2 tsp
Onions, chopped	350 g/1 ¾ cup
Garlic, chopped	10 g/2 tsp
Tamarind pulp	20 g/1 tbsp

Cumin seeds/jeera	5 g/1 tsp
Coriander seeds/dhania	5 g/1 tsp
Mustard oil	50 ml/¼ cup
Sugar	20 g/1 tbsp
Water	1 liter/1 quart
Ghee	10 g/2 tsp (optional)

Wash and dry the eggplants. Leave the stems on and cut them from the base upward into quarters up to three-fourths of the way. This will keep the eggplant together while it cooks. Rub it, inside and out, with some salt, half the turmeric and half the chili powder. Heat the frying oil. When it is hot, lower the eggplants in one at a time (to prevent the oil from splashing) and fry until they are golden. Remove and allow the excess oil to drain.

Blend the tamarind pulp with one cup of hot water, strain, and reserve.

Heat the mustard oil until it smokes. Add the chopped onions. Sauté until golden brown. Add the remaining chili powder and turmeric. Add the chopped garlic and some salt. Cook for five minutes, stirring continuously. When the oil separates from the paste, add the water and the tamarind pulp and stir continuously.

The liquid will thicken as it reaches a boil. When it boils, gently lower the eggplant into it, stirring gently to prevent the eggplant from breaking up. Reduce to a simmer and add the sugar. After about ten minutes the sauce will begin to coat the eggplant. Check the seasoning. Drizzle with ghee and serve hot.

Eggplant Cooked with Margosa Leaves
Neem Begun

Neem leaves have always held an importance in ayurveda and Indian culture for its purported medicinal qualities. They are available at most Indian stores. At first I thought that margosa and eggplant would not be a good pairing, but when my tutor insisted I should, I tried it. Tender, young neem leaves provide a unique flavor to the eggplant. The refreshing sensation of the leaves combines with the earthiness of the eggplant to create a result that is unique and delightful.

Eggplant, diced	150 g/¾ cup
Tender margosa/neem leaves	20 g/1 tbsp
Mustard oil	40 ml/2 tbsp
Salt	5 g/1 tsp
Chili powder	5 g/1 tsp
Ginger, chopped	5 g/1 tsp

Heat the mustard oil in a heavy-bottomed pan until it smokes. Remove from heat for about five minutes to allow the hot oil to cool. Add half the margosa leaves. When they begin to change color, add the diced eggplant, salt, chili and ginger. Simmer over low heat for about ten minutes, stirring occasionally until the eggplant has almost cooked through. Add the remaining margosa leaves, finish cooking, taste, and adjust the seasoning. Serve hot with steamed Basmati rice.

Mixed Vegetables

Turmeric-Perfumed Vegetables
Sukha Sabzi Masala

Peeled potatoes cut into quarters	200 g/1 cup
Peeled carrots cut into ½-inch thick sticks	150 g/¾ cup
Cabbage cut into 1-inch cubes	150 g/¾ cup
Oil	40 ml/2 tbsp
Cumin seeds	5 g/1 tsp
Garlic, roughly chopped	10 g/2 tsp
Fresh chilis, chopped	10 g/2 tsp
Turmeric	20 g/1 tbsp
Salt	to taste
Coriander leaves, chopped	5 g/1 tsp

Heat the oil in a heavy-bottomed pan. Add the cumin seeds until they crackle, then add the potatoes. Toss them until they begin to brown, add the carrots, garlic, fresh chilis, turmeric, and salt and stir for a minute. Add the cabbage and 1/3 cup of water and simmer until the vegetables soften and most of the liquid has been absorbed. Sprinkle in the chopped coriander leaves, stir a couple of times, taste and adjust the seasonings, if required, and serve hot.

Stir-Fried Cabbage with Mustard Seeds and Coconut
Cabbage Foogath

Cabbage, finely shredded	450 g/1 lb
Oil	40 ml/2 tbsp
Mustard seeds	a pinch

Red chilis, dried	5 g/1 tsp
Turmeric	5 g/1 tsp
Fresh chilis, chopped	5 g/1 tsp
Sugar	a pinch
Fresh coconut, grated or desiccated coconut, grated	50 g/¼ cup
Salt	to taste

Heat the oil in a heavy-bottomed pan, adding the mustard seeds and dried red chilis. When the seeds crackle, add the cabbage, turmeric, chopped fresh chilis, sugar, and salt. Stir-fry on high heat until the cabbage is soft. Add the coconut, taste and adjust seasoning, if required, and serve hot.

Mushrooms and Roasted Coconut Curry

Mushroom Xacuti

Xacuti (pronounced Shakootee) is a traditional Goan curry that combines ingredients and spices generally found near the coast.

Mushrooms, sliced	400 g/2 cups
Onions, sliced	100 g/½ cup
Coconut, grated fresh or desiccated	70 g/⅓ cup
Garlic cloves, peeled	10 g/2 tsp
Ginger, peeled and sliced	10 g/2 tsp
Red chilis, dried	20 g/1 tbsp
Mace	a pinch
Black peppercorns	5 g/1 tsp
Cumin seeds	5 g/1 tsp
Cinnamon sticks	2 pieces, about 2–3 inches in length
Cloves	5 buds
Green cardamom	5 pods
Star anise	2
Coriander seeds	a pinch
Turmeric	5 g/1 tsp
Poppy seeds	50 g/¼ cup

Tamarind pulp	40 g/2 tbsp
Oil	40 ml/2 tbsp
Sugar	a pinch
Salt	to taste

In a dry, hot pan, individually roast (see *Tip* below) the onions (until they are golden), coconut, garlic, ginger, dried chilis, mace, black peppercorns, cumin, cinnamon, cloves, green cardamom, star anise, coriander seeds and the poppy seeds until they each change color and release their flavors. Grind all the roasted spices together in a food processor adding enough water to make a smooth paste.

Heat the oil in a heavy-bottomed pan. Add the ground spice paste and stir over low heat until the oil separates from the mixture. Add the sliced mushrooms, turmeric, tamarind pulp, and salt and continue to simmer for twenty minutes or until the mushrooms are cooked through. Stir in the sugar, taste and adjust the seasoning, if required. Serve hot with white rice.

Tip: Because the spices used in this preparation are of differing sizes and of varying characteristics, they are best dry-roasted in hot pans before pounding them together. It does not mean that you need fourteen pans. You simply use a pan to roast one type of spice at a time before keeping it aside to prevent some from burning were they roasted together.

Vegetable Stew with Bengal Gram Dumplings

Gujarati Undhiyo

An undhiyo is a traditional Gujarati dish that has traversed boundaries to become one of the finest exports from that region. This stew is a pleasant melange of rich, earthy flavors.

The muthiyas, the dumplings that are a key component of this dish are named after their method of preparation. The word is derived from the Hindi word muthi which defines a clenched fist, which is what is required to shape them.

Ginger, peeled	20 g/1 tbsp
Garlic cloves, peeled	20 g/1 tbsp
Fresh chilis	10 g/2 tsp

Salt	to taste
Mustard seeds	5 g/1 tsp
Asafoetida	5 g/1 tsp
Small potatoes, peeled	250 g/1 ¼ cup
Baby eggplants	150 g/¾ cup
Broad beans, stringed and diced	100 g/½ cup
Yam, diced	100 g/½ cup
Green plantain, diced	150 g/¾ cup
Turmeric	10 g/2 tsp
Oil	40 ml/2 tbsp
Coriander leaves, chopped	10 g/2 tsp
Coconut, grated fresh or dessicated	40 g/2 tbsp

For the muthiya (dumplings)

Bengal gram flour	50 g/¼ cup
Fenugreek leaves	50 g/¼ cup
Ginger, chopped	5 g/1 tsp
Fresh chilis, chopped	5 g/1 tsp
Oil	to deep fry
Salt	to taste

Make the muthiyas by kneading together the gram flour, fenugreek, ginger, fresh chilis and salt with enough water to make a firm dough. Roll the dough out into sausage lengths the thickness of a pinky finger. Break off inch-long pieces and squeeze each gently in your fist. Deep fry them in hot oil until they are golden. Remove with a slotted spoon and drain the excess oil on kitchen paper towelling or brown kraft paper. Reserve for later use.

Grind the ginger, garlic, and fresh chilis to a paste and reserve.

Cut the eggplant lengthwise into quarters three-quarters through, retaining the stem to make sure that they do not fall apart.

Heat the oil in a heavy-bottomed pan, adding the mustard seeds and asafoetida. When the seeds crackle, add the potatoes and the eggplant. Stir for a minute and add the broad beans and ground spice paste. Sauté on low heat for about ten minutes and stir continuously until the spice mix coats the vegetables. Add the yam and the plantain. Sprinkle in the turmeric and a bit of salt. Stir-fry for about five minutes on high heat. Add 2 cups/400 ml of water.

After bringing to a boil, simmer the vegetables for about ten minutes. Add the fried muthiyas and continue to simmer until the vegetables are tender and the liquid is almost absorbed. Taste and adjust the seasoning, if required. Stir in the coriander leaves and grated coconut and serve hot.

Tip: You may substitute string beans, runner beans or snow peas if broad beans are not available.

Mixed Vegetables with Poppy Seeds
Posto Chorchorri

This is traditionally eaten on lazy Sunday afternoons. It is served with steamed white rice. It is tasty, and exacts its price—a long siesta.

Broad beans (or whole snow peas)	50 g/¼ cup
Baby eggplant, cut as below	70 g/⅓ cup
White radish (daikon), cut into inch-long sticks, ¼-inch thick	50 g/¼ cup
Cauliflower florets, diced small	70 g/⅓ cup
French beans/string beans cut into inch-long sticks	50 g/¼ cup
Poppy seeds	50 g/¼ cup
Fresh chilis	20 g/1 tbsp
Mustard oil	50 ml/¼ cup
Panch phoran (see page 36)	5 g/1 tsp
Dried red chilis, whole	4
Turmeric	10 g/2 tsp
Water	100 ml/½ cup
Salt	to taste

Soak the poppy seeds in ¼ cup of water for at least an hour. Grind them to a paste with the fresh chilis.

Individually fry the vegetables in the hot mustard oil until crisp, remove and drain on absorbent kitchen toweling.

Reheat the oil left in the pan. When it smokes, sprinkle in the panch phoran. When the seeds crackle, reduce the flame adding the dry chilis and stir. Add the poppy seed paste and stir the mixture to prevent it from sticking to the bottom and burning. Cut the eggplant lengthwise into quarters three-fourths of the way up to the stem, retaining the stem so that it holds together. Add ¼ cup of water, salt, and the fried vegetables. Cook until thickened and the vegetables are done. Check and adjust the seasoning. Serve hot.

Tip: Bengalis, the originators of this dish, like to fry their vegetables before simmering them in the sauce. In this way, the vegetables retain some of their crispy texture and do not lose their shape while cooking. While frying the vegetables, take care to fry each kind of vegetable individually. If you fry them together, some may burn before the others even have a chance to change color.

Bengali Pumpkin and Eggplant Stew
Chor Chorri

This is probably one of the most perfect vegetable stews I ever have had. When I say perfect, I mean the balance of flavors, the contrast of textures, and the inter-relationship of spices that bring this dish alive.

Mustard oil	20 ml/1 tbsp
Panch phoran (see page 36)	5 g/1 tsp
White radish/daikon, diced	150 g/¾ cup
Pumpkin, diced	200 g/1 cup
Salt	to taste
Turmeric–	5 g/1 tsp
Eggplant, diced	150 g/¾ cup
Sugar	20 g/1 tbsp
Spinach leaves, washed and trimmed	225 g/½ lb
Red chilis, dried	4

Heat the mustard oil in a heavy-bottomed pan. When it smokes, reduce the flame and add the panch phoran.

When the seeds crackle, add the dried red chilis and the radish and stir briefly. Add the pumpkin, salt, and turmeric.

Simmer while continuously stirring. When the pumpkin begins to soften, add the eggplant and continue to stir.

Check often. When the vegetables are done and the pumpkin appears almost as mashed, check and adjust the seasoning. Add the sugar and spinach leaves. Stir a few times to wilt the spinach and serve hot with rice.

Bengali Stir-Fried Vegetables with Lentil Dumplings
Shukto

Coriander seeds	a pinch
Mustard seeds	a pinch
Ginger, minced	5 g/1 tsp
Ghee	10 g/2 tsp
Bori/sun dried lentil dumplings (optional)	40 g/2 tbsp
Bay leaf	2
Dried red chili	2
Panch Phoran (see page 36)	5 g/1 tsp
White radish, 1-inch-thick slices	50 g/¼ cup
Potato, large cubes	150 g/¾ cup
Plantain, 1-inch-thick slices	150 g/¾ cup
Eggplant, large cubes	150 g/¾ cup
Snow peas	70 g/⅓ cup
Poppy seeds soaked in water for fifteen minutes and ground to a paste	5 g/1 tsp
Milk	150 ml/¾ cup
Whole-wheat flour	50 g/¼ cup
Sugar	20 g/1 tbsp
Chili powder	a pinch
Mustard oil	20 ml/1 tbsp

Grind together the coriander seeds, mustard seeds, and ginger and reserve.

In a heavy-bottomed pot heat the oil and fry the bori until golden. Remove and drain on absorbent paper. In the same oil add the bay leaf, the dried chili and the panch phoran. When the panch phoran crackles add the white radish.

Stir on high heat until the radish changes color and begins to lightly caramelize on the exterior, add the potatoes, plantain, eggplant, and snow peas. Add salt to this and stir regularly on medium heat for five minutes. Add the ginger paste and the poppy seed paste and enough water to cover the vegetables and the fried bori.

In a separate pot, whisk the flour and the milk smooth. Bring this to a slow boil and add the sugar. When the vegetables are tender add this milk-and-flour mixture.

Bring the vegetables to a full boil, then reduce to a simmer for approximately five minutes or until it thickens. Remove from heat and top with the ghee when serving.

Green Mangoes Simmered in Light Mustard Sauce
Ambol

Summers in India are truly hot and bring with them the reward of the mango. During many childhood summers I shinnyed up mango trees to "steal" mangoes. Generally, the owners of the mango trees knew perfectly well who visited their trees at night—it was often their own kids. So long as we weren't egregiously greedy, leaving a sufficient amount of fruit to ripen naturally, we avoided punishment.

Compared to the soft, sweet flesh of the ripened mango, green mangoes are firm-fleshed and tangy. Green mangoes make great pickles and add flavor to stews.

Mustard oil	10 ml/2 tsp
Mustard seeds	5 g/1 tsp
Mustard seeds, ground to a paste with a mortar and pestle	20 g/1 tbsp
Red chilis, dry	2
Turmeric	5 g/1 tsp
Chili powder	a pinch
Salt	to taste
Green Mangoes, peeled, cut into 1-inch cubes	200 g/1 cup

Heat the mustard oil in a heavy-bottomed pan and add the mustard seeds. When the seeds splutter, add the dried chilis, turmeric, chili powder, and salt. Add the mustard paste and stir gently over low heat for a few minutes. Add 100 ml/½ cup of water and the mango pieces and allow them to simmer for about ten minutes. When the pieces are tender and the gravy thickens slightly, taste and adjust seasonings. Remove from the heat and serve hot.

Tip: Green mangoes may be difficult to obtain most of the time. Substitute them with firm, not-quite-ripe ones.

Soya Nuggets Simmered in Maharashtrian Inspired Gravy
Wadiyanche Rassa

Soya nuggets (see *Tip* below)	350 g/1¾ cup
Green chilis	5 g/1 tsp
Garlic	5 g/1 tsp
Turmeric	5 g/1 tsp
Salt	to taste
Copra, grated (see *Tip* below)	120 g/⅝ cup
Coriander seeds	5 g/1 tsp
Dried red chilis, whole	4
Poppy seeds	10 g/2 tsp
Oil	40 ml/2 tbsp
Onion, chopped	50 g/¼ cup
Ginger, shredded	5 g/1 tsp
Cinnamon sticks	2 pieces, about 2–3 inches in length
Green cardamom	4 pods
Bay leaf	1
Chili powder	a pinch
Yogurt, whipped	30 g/2 tbsp
Coriander leaves, chopped	5 g/1 tsp
Juice of one lemon	

Soak the soya nuggets in hot, salted water for about half an hour. Drain and squeeze out excess water. Make a paste of the fresh chilies, garlic, turmeric, and salt and rub this into the nuggets. Let them marinate for half an hour.

Individually pan roast the coconut, coriander seeds, chilis and poppy seeds. Use a mortar and pestle to pound them to a coarse paste adding a little water if needed.

Heat the oil in a heavy-bottomed pan and cook the onions until they are golden. Add the shredded ginger, cinnamon, cardamom, and bay leaf. Stir for a few minutes until the spices begin to change color. Add the marinated soya nuggets, chili powder, and some salt. Continuously stir to prevent the onions from burning. Add the ground coconut paste, stir a few times and add 2 cups of water. Reduce the heat to a simmer. As the gravy thickens stir in the whipped yogurt and continue simmering for ten more minutes to eliminate the raw flavor of the spices. Check and adjust the seasoning, if necessary. Stir in chopped coriander leaves and serve hot with white rice.

Tips: Copra is the sun-dried flesh of the coconut. As the moisture has been evaporated it will keep well for six months without refrigeration. If copra is not available, desiccated coconut can be used instead.

Soya nuggets are texturized vegetable protein known commonly as TVP. They are available at many Indian provision stores in two forms—nugget chunks and granules. It can also be found at health food stores and larger supermarkets.

This recipe states to serve it with rice. There are no rules about when to serve bread and when to serve rice (or both together, for that matter) but some dishes are enhanced when served over rice. This is one of those. (However, the choice is always yours to make.)

Vegetable Dip and Relish
Cheencheeda

Many professional chefs use a variation of this dip for important events like weddings and festivals. While simple to prepare, the blend of different flavors and the multiple senses they affect may make your guests feel you have gone to great lengths to prepare it for them. It is so versatile that it can be eaten as a dip, served as a relish, or substituted for a vegetable side dish.

Turmeric	a pinch
Salt	to taste
Potatoes, peeled and chopped	150 g/¾ cup
Carrots, chopped	40 g/2 tbsp
Green peas	20 g/1 tbsp
Fresh chilis, seeds and stalks removed	10 g/2 tsp
Garlic cloves, peeled	20 g/1 tbsp
Ginger, peeled	10 g/2 tsp
Mustard oil	50 ml/¼ cup
Lemon juice	20 ml/1 tbsp
Coriander leaves, chopped	5 g/1 tsp
Chaat masala (see page 49)	a pinch

Bring the potatoes to a boil in a pot of salted water to which the turmeric has been added. After five minutes, add the carrots, green peas, chilis, garlic, and ginger adding sufficient water to cover. When the vegetables are soft, remove them from the water with a slotted spoon and blend in a food processor to a fine, smooth paste. If they do not blend easily, add back some of the liquid they were boiled in to assist in the process. Remove the blended vegetables to a bowl and gently whisk in the mustard oil, lemon juice, coriander leaves and chaat masala. Taste and adjust seasoning if required. Serve warm or at room temperature.

Rajasthani Wheat Gluten Stew
Chakki ki Subzi

Rajasthan is found in all basic travel guides to India. It has a colorful history enriched by the existence of countless forts, palaces, mahals, and fables.

Rajasthanis are a hardy lot, a basic requirement in dealing with the extreme weather conditions of the Thar Desert. They have survived numerous military campaigns, incursions, and invasions. That they live a life of peace in an insensitive and unyielding land is a true wonder.

In an arid desert, where almost nothing survives the heat, innovation abounds. This nourishing dish is created almost only with gluten. The name refers to a flour mill, called a chakki in Hindi, the source of the main ingredient for this hearty dish.

For the Chakki

Whole wheat flour	3 kgs/6 ½ lbs
Water	as required
Red chili powder	20 g/1 tbsp
Turmeric	10 g/½ tbsp
Oil	10 ml/½ tbsp
Salt	to taste
Oil	to deep fry

For the gravy

Oil	20 ml/1 tbsp
Chopped onions	200 g/1 cup
Ginger paste	5 g/1 tsp
Garlic paste	5 g/1 tsp
Cloves	2
Cinnamon stick	1 piece, about 2–3 inches in length
Green cardamom	4 pods
Black cardamom	1 pod
Red chili powder	20 g/1 tbsp
Coriander powder	10 g/½ tbsp
Turmeric	10 g/½ tbsp
Thick yogurt	60 g/3 tbsp
Grated paneer	30 g/1 ½ tbsp
Water	150 ml/¾ cup
Chopped coriander leaves	10 g/½ tbsp

Make a stiff dough of flour and water. Cover it with a damp cloth and keep it in a cool place for twenty minutes.

Gluten is the sticky part of the wheat grain. As one does not come across it in normal kitchen life, I will do my best to explain how to get to it and what it looks and feels like.

Gluten is the firm sticky material that remains in your hand upon washing away the flour. It resembles the stickiness of a glue stick and has the firmness of freshly kneaded stiff dough. It is arrived at in a process that involves the washing of balls of dough several times. In six and a half pounds of flour, this results in a yield of little more than a cupful of gluten depending on the strength of the flour.

Make golf ball-sized balls of stiff dough by mixing with water. Dip each in a large bowl of water, squeezing repeatedly until the flour is washed off and just the sticky gluten remains.

Add the chili and turmeric, salt, and oil to the gluten and mix well. Spread the gluten on a flat tray to about one-inch thick and steam the lot for approximately 45 minutes. Cut them into inch-sized cubes and deep fry them until they are golden brown. Remove with a slotted spoon and let the excess oil drain onto paper kitchen toweling.

To make the sauce, heat the oil in a pan, adding the onions, garlic, ginger, cloves, cinnamon, cardamom and black cardamom. Over high heat, fry until the spices swell up and begin to change color.

Add the chili, coriander and turmeric powders, the yogurt, paneer, and water. Simmer for fifteen minutes and bring the sauce to a boil for the final minute. Lower the heat and add the gluten dumplings. Simmer until the sauce thickens. Taste and adjust seasonings, if required. Finish with chopped coriander leaves.

For most American cooks this will be a new experience. As you discover methods that make this task simpler for you please share them with me and I will pass them along on our website, www.chefzubin.com. Write to me at zubin@chefzubin.com.

Rajasthani Style Corn Meal Dumplings with Onions and Paneer
Makkai ka Gutta

Corn meal/makkai ka atta	200 g/1 cup
Salt	to taste
Chili powder	5 g/1 tsp
Turmeric	5 g/1 tsp
Water	as required
Oil	20 g/1 tbsp
Cumin seeds	5 g/1 tsp
Fresh chilis, slit (see page 29)	10 g/2 tsp

Coriander leaves, chopped	20 g/1 tbsp
Onions, chopped	150 g/¾ cup
Paneer, grated	50 g/¼ cup
Ginger paste (see page 38)	20 g/1 tbsp

Sift the corn meal. Add the salt, chili powder, and turmeric.

Add water in small amounts. Knead to make a stiff, pliable dough. Roll into cylinders about an inch thick of convenient length, say 6 inches. Add the dough to boiling salted water until they rise to the surface. (Stir the pot a minute or so after adding the dough in case some of the dough should stick to the bottom, preventing their rising.) Boil for five more minutes after they have risen to the surface. Cool the dough and cut into inch long pieces.

Heat oil in a heavy-bottomed pan, until the cumin seeds crackle. Add the onions. When they brown, stir in the ginger paste. Reduce the heat to prevent the ginger paste from burning. Add the fresh chilis and corn dumplings. Toss a couple of times until the onion coats the dumplings and they have reheated. Finish by sprinkling with coriander leaves and grated paneer. Taste and adjust seasoning. Serve hot.

Tips: squeezing some fresh lemon juice on top adds sparkle to the dish.

Grating a store-bought semi-hard or hard cheese over the dish instead of paneer works nicely. Parmesan, though decidedly not Indian, produces great results.

Beetroot and Toasted Sesame Seed Salad

Chukandar aur Til ka Salad

Beetroot	300 g/1 ½ cups
Sesame seeds	30 g/1 ½ tbsp
Mustard seeds	10 g/2 tsp
Fresh chilies	10 g/2 tsp
Ginger, chopped	15 g/3 tsp
Lemon juice	10 ml/2 tsp
Tomatoes, chopped	50 g/¼ cup

| Salt | to taste |
| Coriander leaves, chopped | 5 g/1 tsp |

Boil the beets until they are soft. Peel and slice them and reserve.

Toast the sesame seeds in a hot, dry pan until they are golden. Remove from heat and keep aside.

Soak the mustard seeds in warm water for fifteen minutes and grind them coarsely in a food processor along with the fresh chillies. To this blend, add 50g/¼ cup of the beetroot with ginger, lemon juice, and salt.

Add this to the sliced beetroots along with the chopped tomatoes and more salt if necessary. Taste and adjust the seasoning if necessary. Sprinkle on the sesame seeds and coriander leaves and serve.

Mushrooms Tossed With Corn Kernels and Green Peas

Dhingri Makai Matar

Button mushrooms, sliced (or larger mushrooms, sliced)	400 g/2 cups
Corn kernels	200 g/1 cup
Green peas	100 g/½ cup
Cashew nuts	50 g/¼ cup
Oil	30 ml/1½ tbsp
Cumin seeds	a pinch
Coriander seeds	a pinch
Tomatoes, chopped	150 g/¾ cup
Green chilies, chopped	10 g 2 tsp
Ginger chopped	15 g/3 tsp
Salt	to taste
Coriander leaves, chopped	10 g/2 tsp
Juice of one lemon	

Soak the cashew nuts in warm water for twenty minutes and then grind them to a fine paste.

Heat the oil in a heavy-bottomed pot and add the cumin and coriander seeds. When they crackle, add the mushrooms and stir them on medium heat for a few minutes until they are soft. Add the corn and continue to stir for two more minutes. Add the tomatoes, chilies, and ginger and simmer until the tomatoes become pulpy. Add the cashew nut paste, salt, green peas, and 100 ml/½ cup of water, simmering until the sauce thickens and coats the vegetables. Taste and adjust the seasonings, if required. Remove from the heat and stir in the coriander leaves and lemon juice. Serve hot.

Mushrooms Simmered in a Creamy Saffron-Nut Sauce

Shahi Khumb

Button mushrooms, washed and cut in half (or larger mushrooms, sliced)	800 g/ 4 cups
Oil	30 ml/1½ tbsp
Cumin seeds	a pinch
Onions, sliced	100 g/1 cup
Cashew nuts	50 g/¼ cup
Ginger, chopped	20 g/1 tbsp
Green chilies, chopped	20 g/1 tbsp
Ghee	30 g/ 1 ½ tbsp
Cardamom	6 pods
Cinnamon stick	1 piece, about 2–3 inches in length
Cloves	4 buds
Bay leaf	1
Salt	to taste
Black peppercorns, crushed	10 g/2 tsp
Cream	50 ml/¼ cup

Heat the oil in a heavy-bottomed pot and add the cumin seeds. When they crackle, add the onions, cashew nuts, ginger, and fresh chilies. Stir for a few minutes and then add 400 ml/2 cups of water and bring the mixture to a boil and allow it to boil for a few more minutes. Remove from the heat and cool. Grind the mixture to a fine paste in a food processor.

Heat the ghee in a heavy-bottomed pot. Add the cardamom, cinnamon, cloves, and bay leaf. Add the onion mixture and stir for a few minutes until it takes on a darker hue. Add the mushrooms and simmer until they begin to turn soft. Add the salt, pepper, and 200 ml/1 cup of water and simmer for a few minutes. Taste and adjust the seasonings, if necessary. If the sauce is too thick, add more water and bring it to a boil to adjust the consistency to your liking. Add the cream, bring the sauce to a rapid boil and remove from the heat and serve.

Lentils

The main reason that lentils are so widely used throughout the world is due to their amazing protein content. Lentils, which belong to the legume family, is an amazing twenty six percent protein, making it, along with soya beans, one of the most important in vegetarian uses.

Lest you think that all this fuss is made merely for its protein content, lentils also contain dietary fiber, cholesterol-fighting soluble fiber, iron, folates, Vitamin B1 and minerals.

Lentils were first grown around the Neolithic period. It was one of the first crops to be domesticated in India from where it spread to the rest of the world. India produces half the world's lentil crop with a majority of that being used in its own domestic market.

While Indians refer to all dried beans as "lentils," Americans have a bean specifically called lentil. Lentils are but one kind of dal. The types of lentils/dals used in Indian cooking are:

Lobhia Black eyed peas

Choley/Chana Garbanzo beans, Bengal gram

Rajmah Red kidney beans, available in small and large size and in a variety of colors that range from speckled pink to almost wine-red.

Kala Chana Unpolished black chickpeas

Moong dal When whole they are tiny, green in color, and cylindrically shaped. When they are hulled and split they are tiny, yellow, and almost rectangular in shape. When whole, they are ideal for turning into sprouts with which one can make great salads and sensational stir-fries.

Urad dal When whole these are small, black and cylindrical. When polished and split they are whitish in color.

Chana dal These are yellow and round in shape when hulled and split. They are the largest of the dals.

Arhar /Tuvar dal These are round and dull yellow when hulled and split. They have a matte metallic color when whole.

Masoor Dal These almost look like Tuvar dal except that they are light salmon pink in color.

Dals are one of the most versatile of things to cook. They are tasty, nutritious and can be used in a wide variety of preparations. They must be washed well before use, if not they spoil easily after cooking and, unwashed, give an unpleasant metallic taste to the food.

Bengal gram are garbanzo beans, (also called chickpeas and ceci). The ground beans (gram means beans) is thus referred to as garbanzo bean flour, chickpea flour or, among Indians, besan.

Must is a powdery substance that coats grape skins, lentils, and other things in nature. It is what helps grapes to ferment into wine. However, if it is left on lentils it lends a metallic taste and peculiar odor to the dish. Also, when lentils are not washed well, the finished product tends to spoil faster since, like with wine, there is a similar fermentation process that takes place.

Lentils cook extremely well and much faster in a pressure cooker. Exercise the usual care in their use by following the instructions that came with your cooker.

Tempered Yellow Lentils
Dal Tadka

Ghee	5 g/1 tsp
Cumin seeds	a pinch
Masoor dal	50 g/¼ cup
Turmeric	a pinch
Salt	to taste
Fresh chili, slit (see page 29)	1
Water	300 ml/1 ½ cups
Oil	5 ml/1 tsp
Mustard seeds	a pinch
Red chili, dried	1
Coriander leaves, chopped	5 g/1 tsp

Wash the lentils in running water a few times and drain.

In a heavy-bottomed pot, heat the ghee and add the cumin seeds. When the seeds crackle, add the lentils and stir until they become opaque. Add the turmeric, salt and the slit green chili. Stir for two more minutes and then add about 300 ml (1½ cups) of water.

Reduce the heat and simmer the lentils for fifteen minutes until they are soft and appear mashed. Taste and adjust the seasoning, if required.

In a heavy-bottomed pan, heat the oil and add the mustard seeds and dried chili. When the seeds crackle, pour the oil-spice mixture over the lentils. Finish with chopped coriander leaves and serve hot.

Stewed Whole Black Lentils

Dal Makhani

Black urad dal, whole	100 g/½ cup
Red kidney beans/rajma	40 g/2 tbsp
Ginger, peeled and coarsely crushed	10 g/2 tsp
Garlic, chopped	10 g/2 tsp
Tomatoes, chopped	100 g/½ cup
Tomato paste	20 g/1 tbsp
Green cardamom	6 pods
Chili powder	10 g/2 tsp
Fresh chilis, slit (see page 29)	2
Butter	100 g/½ cup
Heavy cream	50 ml/¼ cup
Salt	to taste
Coriander leaves, chopped	5 g/1 tsp

Clean and wash the lentils. Place them in a pot and cover with ten times the amount of water. Bring to a boil along with the ginger, slit green chilis, cardamom pods and a bit of salt. Boil until the lentils are soft, which is a process that should take about twenty-five minutes. Remove from heat. Discard the cardamom pods, green chilis and ginger. (Stopping cooking at this point makes it easier to find the cardamom before it turns into a mushy mash.)

Heat the butter in a pan and add the chopped garlic. When the garlic begins to change color, add the tomato paste. Stir continuously to prevent the paste from sticking to the bottom of the pan. Add the lentils with their cooking liquid, chili powder, tomatoes, and salt. Mash some of the lentils on the side of the pot and then mix them in to help thicken the dish. Simmer for at least half an hour until the lentils are soft and the stew is thick. Add the cream and simmer until it thickens further. Stir in chopped coriander leaves and serve hot.

Tip: While we say earlier that oil and ghee are interchangeable, this is yet another slight variant. This dish is called "dal makhani." Makhan means butter in Hindi hence the use of whole butter.

Black Eyed Peas with Coconut
Melgor

Black eyed peas/Lobhia	250 g/1 ¼ cup
Oil	40 ml/2 tbsp
Onions, chopped	70 g/⅓ cup
Ginger, peeled and crushed	5 g/1 tsp
Garlic, chopped	10 g/2 tsp
Cumin powder	a pinch
Turmeric	5 g/1 tsp
Coriander powder	a pinch
Tamarind pulp	5 ml/1 tsp
Grated coconut	200 g/1 cup
Fresh chilis, slit (see page 29)	5
Black Pepper	a pinch
Salt	to taste

Rinse a number of times and then soak the beans overnight in suffiecient water that some will remain after soaking. Heat oil in a thick-bottomed pot and sauté the onions until they are golden. Add the ginger and garlic and cook until the garlic begins to change color. Add the cumin, turmeric, and coriander powders. Stir regularly over low heat.

Drain the beans and add them to the pot. Add the tamarind pulp, some salt, and enough water to cover the top of the beans. Add the slit fresh chilis and simmer for half an hour or longer until the beans are soft. Add the grated coconut and stir while returning the beans to a boil. Reduce heat and simmer for fifteen minutes until the gravy is quite thick. Taste and adjust seasonings, if necessary. Serve hot.

Red Kidney Bean Stew
Rajmah Masala

This dish is called 'Rajma-Chawal' when served with rice. It is a favorite in the north.

Sunflower oil	20 ml/1 tbsp
Cinnamon sticks	2 pieces, about 2–3 inches in length
Green cardamom	3 pods
Cloves	3 buds
Onion, chopped	100 g/½ cup
Tomatoes, chopped	150 g/⅓ cup
Red kidney beans	350 g/1 ¾ cup
Garlic, chopped	5 g/1 tsp
Chili powder	a pinch
Turmeric–	10 g/2 tsp
Fresh chilis, slit (see page 29)	3
Ginger, very fine shreds	10 g/2 tsp
Ghee	10 g/2 tsp (optional)
Green coriander leaves, chopped	10 g/2 tsp
Salt	to taste

Soak the kidney beans for about four hours in water sufficient to cover them. This will reduce the cooking time.

In a heavy-bottomed pot, heat the oil and add the cinnamon, cardamom, and cloves. When the spices crackle and begin to swell add the onions and sauté them on low heat until browned.

Add the tomatoes and cook until they are pulpy. Rinse the beans well a number of times. Drain and add them with the chopped garlic, chili powder, turmeric, and slit fresh chilis.

Stir regularly to prevent the mixture from sticking. Add approximately 750 ml/3½ cups of water to the mixture.

Cover loosely and cook at a simmer, stirring occasionally, for half an hour. When the beans are almost done, stir in the salt and continue cooking until done. Add water as necessary to complete the cooking. Remove from the heat and stir in the ginger, ghee, and chopped green coriander.

Serve hot with rice.

Lentil Dumplings in Spiced Ginger Gravy
Dhokar Dalna

Bengal gram/garbanzo beans (soaked for 4–5 hrs)	200 g/1 cup
Oil	20 ml/1 tbsp
Asafoetida	5 g/1 tsp
Ginger	5 g/1 tsp
Garlic, peeled	5 g/1 tsp
Fresh chilli, chopped	2
Mustard oil	40 ml/2 tbsp
Bay leaf	2
Coriander seeds	a pinch
Cumin seeds	a pinch
Turmeric	5 g/1 tsp
Tomatoes, chopped	100 g/½ cup
Red chili, dry	2
Sugar	10 g/2 tsp
Ghee, (optional)	10 g/2 tsp
Coriander leaves, chopped	10 g/2 tsp
Salt	to taste

Rinse a number of times, drain, and process the soaked Bengal gram to a paste. In a heavy-bottomed pot heat oil and stir in the asafoetida. When it changes color, add the ground gram paste and simmer while stirring often for about fifteen minutes, until it thickens. Pour into an inch-deep greased tray (sized so that the contents will be just below the top; i.e., nearly an inch thick) and cool. Cut into bite-sized pieces and deep fry until they are golden and crisp.

With a mortar and pestle, pound together the ginger, garlic and fresh chilli. Reserve.

Heat the mustard oil in a heavy-bottomed pot and add the bay leaf, coriander and cumin seeds, turmeric, red chili, tomatoes, and the pounded chili mixture. When the oil separates and rises from the sides, add 100 ml/½ cup of water and the sugar. When the water comes to a boil, add the fried lentil pieces and boil for two minutes to heat the dumplings. Taste and adjust seasoning, if necessary. Top with ghee and the chopped coriander leaves.

Split Green Lentils with Coconut
Bhaja Moong Dal Narkol Diye

Split green gram/Moong dal	200 g/1 cup
Sugar	10 g/2 tsp
Salt	to taste
Turmeric	5 g/1 tsp
Chili powder	5 g/1 tsp
Oil	20 ml/1 tbsp
Bay leaf	2
Cloves	5 buds
Green cardamom	5 pods
Cinnamon stick	1 piece, about 2–3 inches in length
Dried red chili, whole	4
Cumin seeds	5 g/1 tsp
Coconut, grated fresh	20 g/1 tbsp

Boil the lentils with sugar, salt, turmeric, and chili powder for fifteen minutes or until they are soft. Drain and reserve the lentils. Discard the cooking water.

In a heavy-bottomed pan, heat the oil. Add the bay leaves, cloves, cardamom, cinnamon, and whole chili. When the spices splutter, add the boiled lentils and stir over low heat for two minutes. Add water (about 1 cup/200ml) to adjust the lentils to a flowing consistency.

Check and adjust the seasoning, if necessary. Bring to a boil. Remove from the heat, stir in the grated fresh coconut, and serve hot.

Lentil Dumplings in Mustard Sauce
Bodar Jhal

Masoor dal	250 g/1 ¼ cup
Urad dal	50 g/¼ cup
Fresh chili, chopped	2
Salt	to taste
Mustard oil	70 ml/to ½-inch depth in pan
Mustard seeds	20 g/1 tbsp
Fresh chili	3
Turmeric	10 g/2 tsp
Sugar	5 g/1 tsp
Tomatoes, fresh, pureed	50 g/¼ cup

Soak the lentils in water for about an hour to soften them. Drain. Grind in a food processor, adding water, if necessary, to a quite thick batter. Add the chopped fresh chilis and salt. Work the batter a bit with your hands to make it fluffy.

In a heavy-bottomed pan, heat the mustard oil to frying temperature. When hot, spoon in the lentil mixture, one dollop at a time to form evenly-sized dumplings. Fry on both sides turning them until they are evenly golden. Remove and drain on absorbent kitchen toweling.

Soak the mustard seeds in warm water for about fifteen minutes. Drain and grind to a thick paste along with the fresh chili.

Reheat the remaining oil, add the tomato puree, and stir for a few minutes. Add the mustard paste, chili powder, and turmeric. Simmer and add 150 ml/¾ cup of water and the dumplings. Simmer for ten minutes or so, until the gravy begins to thicken. Bring the sauce to a boil for a minute. When the sauce coats the dumplings, remove from heat and serve hot.

Lentil and Vegetable Stew
Bhaja Moonger Dal

Lentils/Moong dal	150 g/¾ cup
Cauliflower	100 g/½ cup

Green peas	50 g/¼ cup
Potatoes, peeled and cut into cubes	70 g/⅓ cup
Mustard oil (can be substituted)	30 ml/2 tbsp
Cumin seeds/jeera	5 g/1 tsp
Asafoetida	3 g/½ tsp
Bay leaf	2
Green cardamom	2 pods
Clove	4 buds
Cinnamon stick	1 piece, about 2–3 inches in length
Dried red chilis	3
Chili powder	5 g/1 tsp
Salt	to taste
Turmeric	5 g/1 tsp
Sugar	10 g/2 tsp

In a heavy bottomed pot, heat the mustard oil, adding the cauliflower, green peas, and potatoes. Toss until they change color and appear lightly crusted. Remove with a slotted spoon and return the pot to the heat. Add the cumin and asafoetida. After they crackle and turn golden, add the bay leaves, cardamom, cinnamon, chilis, and the lentils (moong dal). Stir on medium heat for two minutes to allow the spices to release their flavor, then add the chili powder and turmeric. Stir for another minute and add the salt, sugar, and enough water to cover the top of the lentils. Reduce the heat to a simmer.

When the lentils are partly done, about ten minutes, add the fried vegetables. Cook for another ten minutes or longer on medium heat until the vegetables and the lentils are soft and the sauce rather thick. Taste and adjust seasonings, if required, and serve hot.

Yellow Lentil and Spinach Stew Flavored with Garlic

Lahsun wali Dal Palak

Ghee–	20 g/1 tbsp
Mustard seeds	a pinch

Cumin seeds	a pinch
Red chili, dried	1
Onion, chopped	40 g/2 tbsp
Moong Dal	150 g/¾ cup
Tomatoes, chopped	50 g/¼ cup
Fresh chilis, chopped	5 g/1 tsp
Turmeric	5 g/1 tsp
Salt	to taste
Spinach leaves, rinsed, and shredded	70 g/⅓ cup
Garlic, chopped	20 g/1 tbsp

Heat the ghee in a heavy-bottom pot. Add the mustard seeds, cumin seeds, and the dried chilis. When the seeds crackle, add the chopped onions and cook until they are golden. Add the lentils and sauté them for a couple of minutes on low heat until they appear almost transparent.

Add the chopped tomatoes, fresh chilis, turmeric, and some salt, continuing to simmer until the tomatoes are pulpy. Add enough water to cover the lentils and bring to a boil for fifteen minutes or until they are soft. Stir occasionally to prevent the lentils from sticking to the bottom. Add water, if necessary, to make a thick stew of pouring consistency. Then, when the lentils are soft and done, add the spinach leaves, and stir for a few minutes to wilt. Taste and adjust the seasoning, if necessary.

Heat the ghee in a pan and cook the garlic in it until it changes color, pour this mix into the lentils and stir until evenly mixed. Serve hot with rice.

Fenugreek Leaves Simmered with Roasted Papad

Papad Pudina ki Subzi

The Marwaris who hail, not surprisingly, from the Marwar region of India had a problem in that they were nomads and vegetarian in the desert. They are a proud bunch who manage always to overcome all obstacles placed before them. This dish is just one example of their indomitable spirit. Its richness in taste belies the sparsity of their lifestyle.

Papads are sun-dried wafers of ground lentil paste. They are readily available at most Indian and Asian provisioners and some supermarkets. They are easy to transport (a boon in the desert) and keep without spoiling for a long time (a boon in the stomach).

Papad	8 pieces
Chopped fenugreek leaves	100 g/½ cup
Mustard oil	20 ml/1 tbsp
Cumin seeds/jeera	a pinch
Fennel seeds/Saunf	a pinch
Chopped onions	100 g/½ cup
Ginger paste	10 g/½ tbsp
Garlic paste	10 g/½ tbsp
Chopped tomatoes	100 g/½ cup
Yogurt, whipped	50 g/¼ cup
Turmeric	5 g/1 tsp
Red chili powder	5 g/1 tsp
Chopped fresh chilis	5 g/1 tsp
Chopped mint leaves	10 g/½ tbsp
Salt	to taste

Spread the papads on a tray and bake in a preheated oven (at 225 C/450 F) for about five minutes until they are evenly golden and crisp. Another way to roast papad is to pop each into a small toaster oven on broil, close to the heat. In about a minute they will pucker and brown. Flip it and do the same to the other side until all the translucent, uncooked areas have become opaque. Yet another way is to use a super-hot cast iron griddleon the range, flipping as with the toaster oven. When baked, reserve for later use.

Heat the oil in a thick-bottomed pot until it smokes. Add the cumin and fennel seeds. When they crackle add the onions and cook them on medium heat until they are golden brown. Add the ginger and garlic paste and stir until it changes color. Add the tomatoes, the fenugreek leaves, and the chopped fresh chilies. Cook until the tomatoes become pulpy. Sprinkle the chili and turmeric powders over the mix, stir a couple of times and simmer for an additional five minutes. Pour in the whipped yogurt and stir gently to create a smooth sauce.

Bring the sauce to a boil for a minute and reduce the heat to a simmer. Break the papad into largish pieces and simmer in the sauce for two minutes. Stir in the mint leaves and serve hot as a side dish with plain white rice.

Bread and Rice

Bread and rice are staples of the Indian diet. Being part of an agrarian culture, Indians rely on a variety of grains.

When the nomadic Aryan culture finally settled in the northern parts of India around 3,500 B.C.E., they established a pattern that altered our dietary habits forever. Although many historians speak of an Aryan invasion, this seems to be a misconception.

The Aryans originally lived in the northern reaches of the subcontinent and led a nomadic existence, herding cattle. Their search for greener pastures led them to the west where, over the years, they added a stay in Europe to their impressive travel itinerary. Faced with going over the huge Caucasus Mountains with their livestock and families, they decided, rather prudently it seems in hindsight, to return to what had come to be home ground. Without modern methods of transport, this journey spanned much time. When they returned to the fertile Hindu Kush valley, they discovered that another culture had settled there in their absence.

The occupiers of Mohenjodaro and Harappa in Pakistan were an agrarian population known as the Dravidians. About 2500 B.C.E., they had well-planned cities with modern plumbing and advanced agricultural techniques—and they were the inventors of the tandoor. Faced with a huge horde of Aryans travelling with hungry cattle that would ultimately destroy their crops, the Dravidians decided to leave their cities and move south where they could preserve their way of life.

Thus two distinct societies began to emerge in India. Given the Dravidian farms and technology, the Aryans decided to trade their nomadic ways and settle down. They found themselves in possession of huge swathes of fertile farmlands as well as several tandoors left behind by the Dravidians. The Dravidians had formerly used their tandoor ovens merely as an alternative to spit-roasting marinated meats. Adding to their bread-making skills, learned in their forays into Europe, the Aryans innovated new varieties of bread using their new-found ovens to create them.

In India, whether rice or bread is served with a meal has more to do with the geographical origins of the diner than their preference.

Northern India has lush wheat fields that often produce record-breaking amounts of grains for the mills that dot our country. They also reap, in smaller quantities, a number of other grains like millet, barley, corn, sorghum, and a grain that is similar to quinoa. The Southern states produce some amount of assorted grains, but a huge quantity of rice.

There are no rules about when to serve bread and when to serve rice. Some dishes are enhanced when served with or over rice. The choice of bread or rice (or both!) is always yours to make.

Asafoetida Enhanced Traditional Bengali Fried Breads

Hinger Kochudi

Bengal gram flour	100 g/½ cup
White flour	100 g/½ cup
Semolina	70 g/⅓ cup
Oil	20 ml/1 tbsp
Turmeric	10 g/2 tsp
Chili powder	10 g/2 tsp
Asafoetida powder/Hing	10 g/2 tsp
Salt	to taste
Oil	to deep fry

In a bowl, knead the gram flour, white flour, semolina, oil, turmeric, chili, asafoetida, and salt with enough water to form a firm dough. Divide the dough into billiard ball-sized balls and keep them covered in a cool place for about half an hour.

Roll the dough into thin, flat discs and fry them in the hot oil until they puff up. Turn them over and continue frying until they are evenly golden. Serve hot with tomato or fruit chutneys.

Rice and Roasted Coconut Flavored Savory Pancakes

Kaltappam

This is a traditional dish from Kerala made during the Lenten season. It is traditional to eat these pancakes on Maundy Thursday, the day that precedes Good Friday. The oldest in the family breaks off bits of the first pancake, distributing it to each member of the family, a tradition reminiscent of the Christian rite of communion and the biblical Last Supper.

Uncooked rice	200 g/1 cup
Urad dal	100 g/½ cup
Oil	25 ml/2 tbsp
Shallots, sliced	30 g/2 tbsp
Coconut, grated	50 g/¼ cup
Cumin seeds, roasted and crushed	5 g/1 tsp
Salt	to taste
Sugar	10 g/2 tsp

Wash and soak the rice and lentils (dal) in separate bowls for at least two hours. Add water to the lentils as they continue to absorb it. Drain and grind the rice and lentils together in a food processor to a fine paste. Cover the bowl with a damp cloth or plastic wrap and keep in a cool place to ferment for at least six hours.

Heat half the oil (1 tbsp) in a heavy-bottomed pan and sauté the shallots until they change color. Add them to the batter with the coconut, cumin seeds, salt, and sugar. In a non-stick pan rubbed gently with oil, ladle a dollop of the batter in the center and gently swirl the ladle on the surface to flatten and expand it to form a 1/3" thick pancake. Flip it and continue to fry on both sides until they are evenly golden. Serve hot.

Fenugreek-Flavored Flat Breads

Methi na Thepla

Fenugreek leaves, finely chopped	50 g/¼ cup
Whole wheat flour/atta	200 g/1 cup

Roasted cumin seeds, crushed to powder	3 g/½ tsp
Turmeric	3 g/½ tsp
Coriander leaves, finely chopped	10 g/2 tsp
Chili powder	5 g/1 tsp
Salt	to taste
Oil for kneading	40 ml/2 tbsp
Oil for basting	20 ml/1 tbsp

Knead together the fenugreek leaves, whole wheat flour, powdered cumin, turmeric, coriander leaves, chili powder, salt, oil, and enough water to make a dough of medium-soft consistency.

Divide the dough into billiard ball-sized balls. Roll them into thin disc shapes. On a griddle or in a griddle pan, toast the dough on either side until it begins to turn golden. Drizzle on a bit of oil and fry until done on both sides. Wipe the griddle clean of crumbs every once in a while. Serve warm or at room temperature with sweet mango chutney. Applesauce is wonderful, too, for an Americanized version, or with a traditional apple chutney.

Fermented Rice and Coconut Batter Pancakes

Appams

This recipe calls for a special appam pan which is available as the traditional cast-iron or a contemporary non-stick version in many Indian stores or from http://showmethecurry.com/catalog/

These are absolutely delicious with a Malabari "ishtew" such as the Kizhanga Ishtew on page 113. This is a dish from Kerala where vegetables are often simmered in coconut milk.

Many Malabaris cannot pronounce the word stew. They live in the lovely lands that form the Malabar Coast. Malabaris and Keralites (who hail from Kerala, a beautiful state of which the Malabar Coast is a part) are charcterized by a rapid-fire manner of speaking. To the casual listener, the Malyalam language sounds as a series of low growly sounds interspersed by a heavily rolled 'o' and 'r'. These characteristics, when moved into other languages promote certain pronunciation difficulties, as in the word "stew."

Appams are eaten with a lightly spiced vegetable and coconut stew. When this was first served to Europeans, they referred to it as "stew." The inhabitants, unable to easily reproduce that sound, have referred to it as an "ishtew" ever since.

Uncooked rice	450 g/1 lb
Sugar	50 g/¼ cup
Dried yeast	20 g/1 tbsp
OR Fresh yeast	10 g/2 tsp
Coconut milk	50 ml/¼ cup
Salt	to taste
Oil	20 ml/1 tbsp (for greasing)

Soak the raw rice in water for at least half an hour, or until the grains are soft. Drain. Grind the rice in a food processor to a fine paste along with the sugar and coconut milk. Add the yeast to the rice batter and allow it to work in a covered bowl in a warm place for one hour.

Lightly grease a non-stick appam pan with oil and heat it on high heat. An appam pan must be used as it ensures that the sides are crisp while the center of the appam is fluffy and moist. When the pan is good and hot and the oil smokes, pour a ladle of the batter into the center of the pan and, lifting the pan, swirl the batter around so that it thinly covers the sides. Reduce the heat to low and cover the pan with a lid. Cook gently for three minutes until the sides are crisp. Remove from the pan and serve hot with the potato "ishtew" on page 113.

Tip: Appams also go well with many other curries or vegetable preparations.

Traditional Whole Wheat Flour Fried Bread

Puri/Poori

Whole wheat flour	500 g/1 lb
Ghee, melted	20 g/1 tbsp
Salt	10 g/2 tsp
Water	300 ml/1 ½ cups (approximately)

| Oil for rolling the dough | 10 ml/2 tsp |
| Oil | for deep-frying |

Sift the flour with the salt. Mix the flour with the ghee to a crumbly texture. Add the water and knead for ten to twelve minutes. Add flour or water as necessary to make a firm dough. Form the dough into golf ball-sized balls.

After the balls have rested for fifteen minutes, use a rolling pin to roll them into ¼-inch-thick flat discs. Dabbing a bit of oil on the dough will facilitate rolling.

Heat the oil in a fryer or round bottomed wok (karahi). When the oil is hot, slide the discs in one at a time. When they puff up, turn them over and fry both sides until they are evenly golden. Serve hot.

Rajasthani Traditional Gram Flour Bread
Missi Roti

Whole wheat flour	150 g/¾ cup
Gram flour	225 g/½ lb
Chili powder	5 g/1 tsp
Fresh chilis, chopped	2
Oil	20 ml/1 tbsp
Ajwain	a pinch
Turmeric	a pinch
Salt	to taste
Ghee	20 ml/1 tbsp

Mix together the whole wheat flour, gram flour, chili powder, turmeric, green chilis, ajwain, and salt. Add the oil and enough water to knead into a firm dough.

Divide the dough into golf ball-sized balls. With a rolling pin, roll out each ball into a ¼-inch-thick, flat disc. Toast on a hot, ungreased griddle plate. When evenly golden, brush with ghee and serve hot.

Gram Flour Savory Pan Breads
Masalaewale Besan ke Rotliyan

These breads are neither rotis nor parathas as similar breads are otherwise named in several parts of India. They look and taste exotic, are quick and easy to prepare, and have a taste that will appeal to most people. They are versatile and may be served with any meal.

Bengal gram flour/Besan	400 g/2 cups
Yogurt	70 g/⅓ cup
Onions, finely chopped	40 g/2 tbsp
Fresh chilis, finely chopped	5 g/1 tsp
Turmeric	5 g/1 tsp
Chili powder	5 g/1 tsp
Coriander leaves, chopped	5 g/1 tsp
Oil	20 ml/1 tbsp
Salt	to taste
Ghee	for frying
Chaat masala (see page 49)	10 g/2 tsp

In a bowl whisk together the gram flour, yogurt, onions, fresh chilis, turmeric, chili powder, coriander leaves, oil, salt, and enough water to make a thick batter of flowing consistency, like breakfast pancake batter.

Heat a non-stick pan and add a teaspoon of ghee. When it sizzles, spoon in enough of the mixture to coat the pan evenly when you roll it about as you would a crepe. Flip it over and cook until both sides are evenly golden. Remove from pan, sprinkle on chaat masala and serve hot. Continue cooking in this manner until all the batter is used up.

Unleavened Griddle-Baked Bread
Chappati

Chappati, also known as phulka, which means "puffed up" (because it puffs up during cooking) is a traditional, unleavened home-cooked bread. Unprocessed whole wheat flour makes it a nutritious offering that can be made even healthier by foregoing the addition of oil to the dough. It is often eaten with dinner because it is light and easily digested.

Whole wheat flour	300 g/1 ½ cups
Oil	20 ml/1 tbsp
Salt	to taste

Sift the flour with salt. Reserve approximately 25 g/2 tbsp of flour. Add the oil and about 150 ml/¾ cups of water to the flour, kneading it until it becomes a soft dough. Form the dough into golf-ball-sized balls and let them rest covered with a damp kitchen towel for half an hour.

Roll the balls out into flat ¼ inch thick discs sprinkling the reserved flour on them to make the rolling easier and bake them on a moderately hot ungreased stovetop cast iron griddle or griddle pan or a non-stick pan, turning them when they are evenly golden and done. Serve hot.

Traditional Whole Wheat and Carom Seed Griddle-Baked Bread
Ajwaini Paratha

Whole wheat flour	300 g/1 ½ cups (plus enough for use in dusting the dough—see below)
Salt	to taste
Carom seeds	a pinch
Ghee	30 g/1 tbsp plus enough to apply to dough—see below
Water	as required

Sift the flour with the salt. Melt the ghee and add 1 tbsp to the flour along with the carom seeds. Gently mix the ghee into the flour with your fingers until the dough becomes crumbly. Slowly add sufficient water (about 150 ml/¾ cup) and knead to form a soft dough. Divide the dough into golf ball-sized balls. Let them rest, covered with a damp kitchen towel, for twenty minutes,

Roll the dough out to a quarter of an inch thickness. Paint a bit of ghee on the entire surface with a pastry brush and dust some flour over it. From one side, pleat the dough into gathered folds. Roll it up across the pleats from one end to the other so that it now resembles a jelly roll. Place the loose end under the dough and continue in the same manner with the rest of the balls. Leave this to rest for about fifteen minutes before rolling them out into flat round discs of roughly a half inch in thickness.

Bake them on moderate heat on a cast iron stovetop griddle or griddle pan or a non stick pan turning when they are evenly golden. Brush a bit of ghee onto the first side, continuing cooking until they are crisp; turn and repeat. Serve hot.

Beetroot and Cardamom Bread
Chukandar ki Roti

Beetroots (Americans call them plain old "beets") are healthy, nutritious, and provide much dietary fiber. The tender shoots are eaten during the summer and the beets themselves, because they are hearty and easily kept, are best consumed during winter. As they are easy to grow, the harvests are generally plentiful and they appear in all kinds of preparations. They can be pickled, dried, or salted to facilitate storage and increase their shelf life.

Beetroot, whole	200 g/equivalent to 1 cup
Green cardamom	10 pods
Whole wheat flour	400 g/2 cups
Oil	15 ml/1 tbsp
Ginger, chopped	10 g/2 tsp
Salt	to taste
Ghee	15 g/1 tbsp

Boil the beets for twenty minutes to soften them. Peel, and puree them in a blender. Pound the cardamom in a mortar with a pestle to obtain a coarse powder. Discard the cardomom husks and add the powdered seeds to the beetroot puree. It may be easier to break open the pod with your fingers and pound the seeds after they are stripped out of the husk.

Mix the flour, oil, ginger, salt, and pureed beets, kneading the mixture thoroughly to form a soft, smooth dough adding water only if necessary. Divide the dough into golf ball-sized balls. Cover these with a damp cloth and rest them in a cool place for half an hour.

Sprinkle a bit of flour on a work table and roll the dough balls out into ¼-inch thick, round discs. Bake them on a hot griddle pan or non-stick pan until they are golden on either side. Brush a bit of the ghee onto each and serve hot.

Savory South Indian Rice and Lentil Pancake

Uttapam

These thick, crisp pancakes are delicious and easy to prepare. Soaking and fermentation requires that its preparation cannot be a spur of the moment decision, but it is an absolute delight to eat and to cook and well worth the effort.

Urad dal	100 g/½ cup
Rice	300 g/1 ½ cup
Salt	to taste
Sugar	5 g/1 tsp
Tomatoes, chopped	40 g/2 tbsp
Onions, chopped	40 g/2 tbsp
Coriander leaves, chopped	10 g/2 tsp
Fresh chilis, chopped	5 g/1 tsp
Cashew nuts, crushed	10 g/2 tsp
Cumin seeds, roasted and powdered in a mortar with pestle	5 g/1 tsp
Oil	20 ml/1 tbsp

Rinse the rice and the lentils and soak them in a bowl for three to four hours to soften them. Process them together in a food processor to a smooth paste. Mix them in a bowl with the sugar and leave in a cool place to ferment for six to eight hours. Mix in the salt and a bit of water, if necessary, to create a fluffy, thick batter of coating consistency.

Use a non-stick pan. Rub the surface with butter or oil to leave a thin coating. Pour enough batter onto the center and gently spread it in concentric circles with the bottom of the ladle to form a thick pancake.

Sprinkle on the chopped tomatoes, onions, coriander leaves, green chilis, cashew nuts, and a bit of roasted cumin powder. Drizzle on a bit of oil and flip over the pancake. Cook it until both sides are golden and crisp

Serve hot. While one may vary the toppings, the classic toppings regularly served are coconut chutney (see page 188) and sambhar (see page 198).

Sorghum Bread
Jwarichi Bhakri

Sorghum is rather hard grain that is grown abundantly in Maharashtra. This bread is "poor man's food," in that its high iron and fibre content help to make up for deficiencies in a poor diet.

Sorghum flour or 'jawar,' as it is commonly known, is available at many Indian provision stores.

Sorghum flour/Jawar flour	500 g/1 lb
Water	200 ml/1 cup (approximately)
Salt	10 g/2 tsp
Butter or ghee (Optional)	15 g/1 tbsp

Knead together the flour, salt, and enough water to make a soft smooth dough. Divide the dough into golf ball-sized balls. Flatten the balls into round discs, about a third of an inch thick with your palms. Bake on medium heat on a cast iron stovetop griddle or griddle pan, or non-stick pan turning until golden on both sides and cooked through. Brush on butter or ghee and serve hot.

Sweet Vegetable Pilaf
Subz Muthanjan Pulao

This pilaf was originally prepared in the royal kitchens of the Mughal emperors with lamb as the main ingredient. Over the years, as alliances were forged with vegetarian Hindu chieftains who had representatives at court and who attended royal banquets, a number of vegetarian dishes were developed.

Sweet, dried fruit-infused rice was meant to provide the diner a melange of tastes when combined with spice-laden curries.

This rice dish is often served on its own as a meal. Served as a side dish this recipe could serve as many as ten people.

Soya nuggets/TVP	300 g/1½ cups
Salt	to taste
Ghee	100 g/½ cup
Cloves	6 buds
Green cardamom	6 pods
Onions, sliced	300 g/1 ½ cup
Ginger, chopped	10 g/2 tsp
Coriander seeds, crushed	20 g/1 tbsp
Carrots, diced	300 g/1 ½ cup
Green peas	60 g/3 tbsp
Sliced mushrooms	60 g/3 tbsp
Milk	2 lt/2 quarts
Almonds, blanched, peeled and sliced	200 g/1 cup
Basmati rice	1 kg/2.2 lb
Raisins	100 g/½ cup
Sultanas (or raisins)	100 g/½ cup

A few strands of saffron dissolved in warm water

Soak the soya nuggets in hot salted water for twenty minutes. Drain and squeeze off the excess water. Reserve.

In a heavy-bottomed pot, heat the ghee, add the cloves and cardamom, cinnamon, cumin, and black peppercorns. When they sizzle and start to change color, add the sliced onions, ginger, and coriander. Sauté until the onions are golden brown. Add the vegetables and stir until they are evenly glazed and gain the sheen that cooking in butter provides. Add the soya nuggets, season with salt and reserve.

Bring the milk to a boil and continue at simmer to reduce the milk to a third of its original volume. Grind half the almonds using a portion of the milk and mix it back into the rest of the milk. Reserve.

Rinse the rice and soak it in water for at least 15 minutes. Drain and reserve.

Bring one and one-half quarts of water to a boil. Add the rice and a bit of salt, reduce the heat to simmer, cover, and cook until the rice has absorbed all of the liquid. This should take about twenty minutes.

In a wide pot spread some of the vegetable-soya mixture. Cover with a third of the rice, pour in a third of the milk and sprinkle in some of the dried fruits and saffron. Repeat this process two more times so that everything is used up.

Cover the pot with a lid and fasten it securely to the sides with aluminium foil all around, to seal it against moisture escaping. Place the pot in a preheated oven at 150*C/300*F for twenty minutes. Remove and open the pot carefully as escaping steam can cause severe burns even at some distance. Serve hot.

TVP (texturized vegetable protein) can be found in health food stores and large supermarkets.

Tip: This style of biryani or cooking, where the steam and the flavors are trapped within, is referred to as Dum. Since the pot is not hermetically sealed, some steam will escape, but this sealing does speed up the cooking process thereby retaining a lot of flavor.

Tomato Rice

A traditional South-Indian rice preparation that is differently flavored and more complex than its Mexican counterpart, it makes for a light and flavorful lunch.

Tomatoes, chopped	200 g/1 cup
Onions, chopped	70 g/⅓ cup
Cloves	4 buds
Mustard seeds	a pinch
Mint leaves, chopped	5 g/1 tsp
Basmati rice	150 g/¾ cup
Oil	20 ml/1 tbsp
Ghee/clarified butter, melted	20 g/1 tbsp
Ginger, peeled	10 g/2 tsp
Garlic cloves, peeled	10 g/2 tsp
Cinnamon stick	1 piece, about 2–3 inches in length
Coconut flesh	40 g/2 tbsp
Red chilis, dried	6
Curry leaves	1 sprig
Turmeric–	5 g/1 tsp
Chopped mint leaves	5 g/1 tsp
Salt	to taste
Sugar	a pinch
Coriander leaves, chopped	5 g/1 tsp

Rinse the rice and soak it in water for about ten minutes.

In a food processor, grind together the ginger, garlic, cinnamon, coconut, dried chilis and a bit of water to obtain a coarse paste. Reserve.

In a heavy-bottomed pan heat the oil and add the mustard seeds and cloves. When the seeds crackle, add the chopped onions. Stir until the onions are soft and appear transparent. Add the curry leaves. When the leaves crackle, add the ground paste, turmeric, and chopped tomatoes. Cook until the tomatoes are pulpy. Add the drained rice and stir for two minutes. When the rice grains are evenly coated with the mixture and begin to appear opaque, add 275 ml/1 1/3 cups of water, salt, sugar, and the mint leaves. Reduce to a simmer, stir a few times, and cover. Stir gently after ten minutes and every two minutes thereafter until the rice is cooked, a process that takes about fifteen minutes.

Drizzle the ghee onto the rice and mix in the chopped coriander leaves with a spoon. Check and adjust seasoning, if required. Remove from heat and serve hot.

Spicy Maharashtrian Fried Rice
Masala bhaat

Basmati rice	100 g/½ cup
Eggplant, (with skin) round slices to dime thickness	150 g/¾ cup
Coriander leaves, chopped	20 g/1 tbsp
Coconut, grated	50 g/¼ cup
Cashew nuts	10
Cloves	4 buds
Cinnamon stick	1 piece, about 2–3 inches in length
Fresh chilis, chopped	2
Yogurt	30 g/2 tbsp
Coriander seeds	5 g/1 tsp
Cumin seeds/jeera	5 g/1 tsp
Mustard seeds	a pinch
Chili powder	a pinch
Turmeric	a pinch
Asafoetida	a pinch

Salt	to taste
Oil	40 ml/2 tbsp

Use a food processor or a mortar and pestle to grind the coriander seeds, cumin seeds, cloves, and cinnamon to a powder.

Rinse the rice, drain, and reserve.

In a thick-bottomed pot heat the oil and add the mustard seeds. When they crackle, add the asafoetida and the turmeric.

Stir continuously to prevent them from burning and sticking to the bottom. When the mixture turns golden, add the eggplant. Sauté on low heat for five minutes. Add the chopped fresh chilis and the rice and sauté while stirring in the salt, chili powder, ground spices, yogurt and the cashew nuts—until the ingredients are well mixed.

Add 200ml/1 cup of boiling water. When the mixture comes again to a boil, reduce the heat to simmer and cook partially covered for around fifteen minutes, until the water has been absorbed and the rice is done.

Garnish with grated coconut and chopped coriander leaves. Serve hot.

Sprouted Moong Bean Pilaf
Moongwali Pulao

Oil	20 ml/1 tbsp
Cumin seeds	a pinch
Green cardamom	4 pods
Cloves	4 buds
Cinnamon stick	1 piece, about 2–3 inches in length
Bay leaf	1
Long grained basmati rice	500 g/1.1 lb
Onions, chopped	50 g/¼ cup
Sprouted (see page 41) moong beans	70 g/⅓ cup
Ginger, shredded	10 g/2 tsp
Cherry tomatoes cut into half	20 whole

Fresh chilis, chopped	5 g/1 tsp
Salt	to taste
Coriander leaves, chopped	5 g/1 tsp

Rinse the rice and soak in water for about ten minutes. Drain and reserve.

In a heavy-bottomed pot, heat the oil and add the cumin seeds, cardamom, cloves, cinnamon, and bay leaf. When the spices begin to change color and swell, add the rice. Add the onions, stirring continuously on low heat until the onions become transparent. Add the bean sprouts and continue stirring for a few more minutes. Add some salt, the ginger and 4 1/2 cups/900 ml of water. Stir a few more times, cover, and simmer on low heat for about twenty minutes until the rice is nearly done.

Stir in the tomatoes and fresh chilis and continue to simmer until the rice is completely done and the liquid has evaporated. Garnish with coriander leaves and serve hot.

Beetroot and Cumin Pilaf
Chukandar pulao

Peeled and chopped beets	200 g/1 cup
Uncooked rice	500 g/2½ cups
Mustard seeds	10 g/2 tsp
Fresh chillies	10 g/2 tsp
Oil	20 ml/1 tbsp
Cumin seeds	5 g/1 tsp
Chopped onions	30 g/1½ tbsp
Chopped ginger	15 g/3 tsp
Salt	to taste
Chopped coriander leaves	5 g/1 tsp

Soak the mustard seeds in hot water for about half an hour and grind to a coarse paste in a food processor along with the fresh chilis.

Heat the oil in a thick-bottomed pot and add the cumin seeds. When they crackle, add the chopped onions and cook them gently until they are golden.

Add the beets, rice, and ground mustard paste and cook on medium heat until the beetroot begins to soften. Add ginger, salt and about 850 ml/4¼ cups of water and simmer the rice, covered, until the rice is done.

Remove from the heat and gently fork in the coriander leaves without mashing the rice. Serve hot with an optional drizzle of melted ghee.

Vegetable, Rice, and Lentil Stew
Khichadi

This dish has been a staple of yogis and sages for at least five thousand years. These wise men usually eat only one meal a day. How wise is this?—very, very wise, and thus they are not very, very wide. One letter, like one meal, can make a great deal of difference!

The meal they generally have is a khichadi. To vary their experience, the kinds and combinations of vegetables and/or lentils is changed.

Ghee	40 g/2 tbsp
Green cardamom	4 pods
Cloves	2 buds
Black peppercorns	4
Cinnamon stick	1 piece, about 2–3 inches in length
Bay leaf	1
Cumin seeds	5 g/1 tsp
Onions, chopped	50 g/¼ cup
Garlic, chopped	5 g/1 tsp
Basmati rice	150 g/¾ cup
Moong Dal /lentils	50 g/¼ cup
Carrots, chopped	40 g/2 tbsp
Mushrooms, chopped	50 g/¼ cup
Potatoes, peeled and diced	40 g/2 tbsp
Turmeric	10 g/2 tsp
Fresh chilis, slit (see page 29)	2
Salt	to taste
Coriander leaves, chopped	5 g/1 tsp

Rinse the lentils and the rice together. Soak in water for fifteen minutes, drain and reserve.

Heat the ghee in a heavy-bottom pot and add the cardamom, cloves, pepper-corns, cinnamon, bay leaf, and cumin. When the spices crackle, add the onions and stir them over moderate heat until they are golden. Add the chopped garlic, rice, and lentils. Continue stirring until the rice appears translucent. Add the vegetables and the turmeric and continue to stir for a couple of minutes to prevent the spices from sticking to the bottom. Add the slit fresh chilis, salt, and 2 cups/400 ml of water. Simmer for twenty five minutes until the rice, lentils, and vegetables are soft and appear almost as mashed and the water has been absorbed. Taste and adjust seasoning, if required. Stir in the coriander leaves and serve hot.

Morel and Saffron Biryani

Zaffrani Gucchi Biryani

This biryani was served in the courts of the Mughal emperors whenever they entertained guests of state or dignitaries of high standing. It is a rich, flavorful, and elegant biryani, a look back at the decadent lifestyle of that era.

Fresh morels are a weonderful albeit expensive treat. Dried morels will work as well as fresh and are available in upscale supermarkets and gourmet stores.

Morels	12
Saffron	a large pinch
Basmati rice	450 g/1 lb
Ghee	50 g/¼ cup
Bay leaves	2
Cinnamon	1 piece, about 2–3 inches in length
Cardamom	4 pods
Cloves	4 buds
Milk	400 ml/2 cups
Onions,chopped	100 g/½ cup
Garlic, chopped	20 g/1 tbsp
Ginger, chopped	20 g/1 tbsp
Tomatoes, chopped	100 g/½ cup
Dried fenugreek leaves/ kasturi methi	10 g/ 2 tsp

Green chilies, chopped	4
Cashew nuts, chopped	20 g/ 1 tbsp
Raisins	20 g/ 1 tbsp
Yogurt	200 g/ 1 cup
Salt	to taste
Mint leaves, chopped	10 g

Wash the morels thoroughly. If they are dried, soak them in warm water for half an hour. Slice the morels and set them aside.

Wash the rice well several times under running water unill the water runs clear.

Add 20 g/1 tbsp of the ghee to a heavy-bottomed pot along with the bay leaves, cinnamon, cardamom, cloves, milk, and 100 ml/½ cup of water. Bring the liquid to a boil, add in the rice and salt, and stir a few times until the liquid comes to a boil again.Cover and reduce the heat to simmer for fifteen minutes until all the liquid has been absorbed by the rice. Remove from the heat and stir gently with a fork to avoid breaking the grains.

Heat the rest of the ghee in a thick-bottomed pot. Add the onions and stir until they are golden. Add the garlic and ginger and, when they turn golden, add the tomatoes, dried fenugreek leaves, chilies, morels, and salt. Stir for a few minutes. Add the cashew nuts and raisins and layer the cooked rice on top of this mix. Sprinkle on the saffron and the yogurt. Place a tight-fitting lid on top and simmer for twelve minutes. Open the lid, stir in the mint leaves gently and serve hot.

Mukhvas

The name of this dish is probably formed from two Gujarati words: Mukh which means mouth and Vas which means smell.

A Mukhvas began as an ancient Indian remedy for bad breath. Indians used a variety of herbal twigs to clean their teeth, giving them shiny pink gums, but this did nothing for the inevitable odor resultant from eating a spice and garlic-infused meal.

Not content with chewing a few sweet spices such as anise seed, the emperors of yore decreed that this was not a fitting tribute to end a lavish meal. This prompted a scramble among the nobles and notables, the physicians and the chefs, each hoping to gain the emperor's favor as well as a few bits from the treasury.

Simple spice mixtures grew in complexity to include even noble metals such as gold and silver, expensive saffron strands, hard-to-come-by exotic spices brought from faraway lands, and whatever the ruling doctors prescribed as healthful at that time.

This process of refining and innovating continues in modern-day India where several varieties of these mouth fresheners are available commercially as well as being prepared in many homes across the country. Such recipes are handed down through the generations.

As one leaves most Indian restaurants in the U.S., you will find a mixture of spices, seeds, and sugar confections in a bowl near the cash register. These are more often than not purchased. They include such seeds as a special kind of sweet fenugreek, mildly fragrant fennel seeds, and bits of spices like cardamom and cloves. You might find tiny chunks of crystallized sugar, sugar coated cumin, and even spiced bits of tamarind or dried betel leaf.

Obviously it is easier to pick up a packet of the readymade stuff than to consider making it yourself.

Spice-Stuffed Dates
Masala Khajoor

These are served as after-dinner mouth fresheners in many parts of India. The spicy, sweet, and tangy flavors combine to give a refreshing coolness.

Dried dates	100 g/½ cup
Cumin seeds	10 g/2 tsp
Dried pomegranate seeds/anardana	50 g/¼ cup
Fennel seeds	10 g/2 tsp
Finely granulated sugar	20 g/1 tbsp
Cinnamon powder	5 g/1 tsp
Aamchur/dried mango powder	10 g/2 tsp
Lemon juice	20 ml/1 tbsp
Rock salt or kosher salt	10 g/2 tsp
Chopped mint leaves	5 g/1 tsp

Using a mortar and pestle, grind the salt to a coarse powder and soak the dates in the salt and lemon juice for a day, at room temperature. Stir every few hours. (It's ok—you're allowed to sleep!) Remove the pits and squeeze away the moisture drawn by the salt.

Roast and grind the cumin seeds, pomegranate, and fennel. Mix together these ground spices with the mango powder and mint leaf. Stuff the mixture into the dates and roll them in a mixture of the sugar and cinnamon. They can be prepared and stored in the refrigerator for a week to ten days.

Tip: Regular table salt can be substituted, but use less.

Rose Petal Jam
Gulkhand

Fresh rose petals can be gotten from most florists. These need not be costly; the ones that fall off the flower and gather at the bottom of the basket are perfect. I have used this recipe, too, with marigold and lavender petals with great results.

This jam is intended to be eaten in small quantities and may be used as a topping on sweetened coconut pancakes and the like.

Rose petals	200 g/1 cup
Honey	60 g/4 tbsp
Juice of one lemon	
Cinnamon sticks	2 pieces, about 2–3 inches in length
Fennel seeds	a pinch
Grated lemon zest	5 g/1 tsp

Rinse the rose petals, dry them with a paper towel and spread them on a tray.

Boil 100 ml/½ cup of water in a pot with the honey, lemon juice, cinnamon and fennel. Skim off the froth that rises to the surface. After a minute or so, stir in the rose petals and simmer for twenty minutes or more until the mixture gets thick. Stir in the lemon zest, taste, and adjust sweetness, if necessary. Remove from heat and chill before serving.

Tip: If the Gulkhand turns too sweet add a bit of lemon juice and lime zest to adjust the taste

Chutneys

In New York and its environs, Indian restaurants often serve a triptych of mint sauce, tamarind sauce, and onion relish with the appetizer course. In India you might instead get mint chutney with lime or mango pickle along with those red pickled onions. The onions are not really meant to be eaten with poppadums, but with the entrée, but I know that Americans find it easier to mount the onion onto the papads—much easier, indeed, than spooning the mint chutney or tamarind sauce onto the papad so it drips onto the tablecloth during transport to the mouth (or dipping the papad into the sauces to avoid that, but then not getting enough of that good stuff becaue it runs off).

And why, if the onions are meant for the entrée, does the waiter clear the chutneys just before the entrée is served? Tell your server that Zubin says the onions are for the entrée and to leave his cotton-picking fingers off the chutneys!

Tamarind and Palm Sugar Chutney
Sonth ki Chutney

Tamarind, concentrate or desiccated	150 g/¾ cup
Palm sugar or white cane sugar	50 g/¼ cup
Ginger, powdered	5 g/1 tsp
Cumin seeds, roasted and powered	5 g/1 tsp
Salt	20 g/1 tbsp
Chili powder	3 g/½ tsp

Boil the tamarind in 4 cups/800 ml of water for half an hour. Remove from heat and let it steep for an additional hour. Pass through a sieve to eliminate the pulp, seeds, and fiber.

Simmer the tamarind liquid extract with the sugar and the other ingredients. Stir until the sugar dissolves. When done, check and adjust the seasonings, if necessary. Ensure that the sauce is thick enough to coat the back of a spoon or thin down with water if necessary. Chill before serving.

Coriander and Mint Leaf Chutney

Dhaniya Pudina ki Chutney

Coriander leaves, not stems	100 g/½ cup
Mint leaves, fresh	100 g/½ cup
Green chilis, stalks removed	8
Tamarind pulp	50 g/¼ cup
Palm sugar or cane sugar	a pinch
Salt—	to taste

In a food processor, process the coriander leaves, mint leaves, green chilis, tamarind pulp, salt, sugar and enough water to make a smooth, thick paste. Check and adjust salt if required and keep refrigerated until it is to be served.

Coriander, Mint Leaf and Yogurt Chutney

Pudina ki Chutney

This is an alternative recipe for mint chutney using yogurt. It is used mainly as a dip when eating samosas or pakoras.

Coriander leaves, no stems	100 g/½ cup
Mint leaves, fresh	100 g/½ cup
Green chilis, stalks removed	8
Whipped yogurt	50 g/¼ cup
Sugar	10 g/2 tsp
Salt	to taste

In a food processor, process the coriander leaves, mint leaves, green chilis, salt, sugar, and enough water to make a smooth, thick paste. In a bowl, whisk the yogurt until it is smooth. Gently whisk in the ground paste until it is evenly incorporated. Check and adjust salt, if required. Keep refrigerated until it is served.

Apple and Raisin Chutney
Saeb aur Kismis ki Chutney

Red apples	450 g/1 lb
Raisins	100 g/½ cup
Oil	30 ml/1½ tbsp
Nigella/kalonji	a pinch
Fennel seeds	a pinch
Chopped fresh chilies	10 g/2 tsp
Chopped ginger	15 g/3 tsp
Turmeric powder	a pinch
Salt	to taste
Chopped mint leaves	10 g/2 tsp

Wash the apples and cut them into ½″ cubes with the skin on. Discard the core and seeds.

Heat the oil in a pan adding the nigella and fennel seeds. When they crackle, add the raisins and stir them round till they begin to soften. Add the apples and stir on high heat for a couple of minutes until the apples begin to soften. Sprinkle in the chilies, ginger, turmeric powder and salt and toss for a minute more. Taste and adjust the seasonings, if necessary. This chutney should be a blend of spicy and sweet tastes. Stir in the mint leaves. Remove from the heat and serve warm.

Coriander and Coconut Chutney

A chutney of south Indian origin that is great to serve with snacks like idlis, dosas, and vadas.

Coconut, grated	5 g/1 tsp
Coriander leaves	5 g/1 tsp
Fresh chillies	20 g/1 tbsp
Tamarind pulp	60 g/3 tbsp
Oil	20 ml/1 tbsp
Mustard seeds	a pinch

Curry leaves	1 sprig
Channa dal	3 g/½ tsp
Red chilis, dry	3
Salt	to taste
Sugar	to taste

In a food processor, process the fresh chilis, coconut, coriander leaves, tamarind pulp, salt, and sugar and a bit of water to a smooth paste. Reserve.

In a thick-bottomed pan, heat the oil and add the mustard seeds and curry leaves. When the seeds splutter, add the lentils and the dried red chilis. When the lentils (dal) begin to change color (in about five minutes) pour the lentils and oil over the prepared chutney paste. Stir with a spoon to ensure that the flavors are evenly mixed. Serve chilled or at room temperature.

Tomato Chutney with Raisins

Tamater Manukaer Chutney

Fresh tomatoes, chopped	200 g/1 cup
Sugar	30 g/2 tbsp
Vinegar	20 ml/1 tbsp
Garlic cloves, chopped	10 g/2 tsp
Ginger, shredded or chopped	10 g/2 tsp
Dried red chillies, chopped	5 g/1 tsp
Fresh chillies, chopped	5 g/1 tsp
Salt	to taste
Raisins	15 g/1 tbsp

Combine all ingredients in a flat-bottomed pan and regularly stir gently for half an hour over low heat. When the mixture begins to thicken, remove from heat and cool. Serve.

Date And Tomato Chutney

Tamatar Khajoorer Chutney

This is a chutney I have found to be wonderful, tasty, and versatile. It can be used as a dip, sauce, accompaniment, or condiment. It is particularly good with steaming hot puris.

Mustard oil	10 ml/2 tsp
Panch phoran (see page 36)	5 g/1 tsp
Chopped tomatoes	200 g/1 cup
Palm sugar or cane sugar	20 g/1 tbsp
Dried red chillies, chopped	2
Deseeded and chopped dates	20 g/1 tbsp
Salt	to taste

In a heavy-bottomed pan, heat the oil until it smokes. Remove from heat and add the panch phoran. When the seeds crackle return to heat and stir in the tomatoes.

Cook the tomatoes for about 10 minutes on moderate heat until they are pulpy. Add in the sugar. Simmer until the sugar dissolves. Add the chilis and cook for a minute longer and taste. Adjust the seasoning or sweetness, if desired. Add the chopped dates. Stir for a couple of minutes, remove and cool.

Refrigerated, this chutney will keep for up to a week.

Chaat

Every country, each place in the world, has a set of culinary characteristics or experiences that make it distinct and sometimes so unique that that place can be identified by its particular uniqueness. The French have bistro food; the English, their pub food; the Portuguese have sausage and beer (as do, differently, the Germans); and the Americans have diner food.

Indians have chaat, a generic term that refers to a grouping of foods that are rather like tapas. Chaat is widely eaten all over India and is available in some form or another in restaurants or street stalls and other eateries. The characteristics of a chaat are that they are small portions, have a melange of sweet, spicy, acidic, and astringent flavors along with crisp, soft or crunchy textures.

Chaat is typified by a ramshackle street stall (derelict, even) manned, perhaps, by a betel leaf-chewing man of less-than-kempt appearance, offering a small tray of assorted ingredients and spiced chutneys. Ignore the teeming crowd before the counter (jostling for prime position is considered good form as it contributes exercise to help work up an appetite) and shout out your order.

The person working the stall moves about with a dexterity and skill that belies his appearance. He is mixing ingredients with chutneys, popping raw onions atop some things, and strands of fresh coriander onto others. He slides these onto sheets torn from glossy old gossip magazines which is handed to you while he rapidly moves on to the next order. Once you've gotten your order move out of the way, lose yourself in the flavors, and go back to do it all over again.

Although there are favorites, given the number of ingredients available on the tray, there are unnumbered possibilities, permutations, and combinations. The Golgappa puris could be filled with sprouted beans and a chilled mint and tamarind water (yes, it's poured in. and quite slurpy) that create the famous "Pani puris" or they may be stuffed with spiced potatoes and topped with savory yogurt to make "Dahi Puris."

Every city, town and village in India has its supply of chaat vendors. It is great fun just to stand around and watch them prepare their food, but better, is having it trigger the neurons in your brain that send out waves of pleasurable sensation at the moment it hits the tip of your tongue.

Much like some of the world's great performance artists or the famous chefs among us, these vendors take great pride in their work, calling out loudly to passers-by to come to partake of their creations; to savor their masterpieces.

Evenings bring throngs to crowd the tiny stalls. Plates are quickly filled, passed around, emptied, and refilled again. Business doesn't slow until the late hours of the night. Many Indian ex-pats yearn not as much for the motherland as for the delights of these culinary artists.

Making chaat at home is relatively easy as most of the ingredients are readily available in grocery stores in Indian or in Indian/Asian stores around the world. Many of the following recipes are components of chaat.

Does eating chaat warrant the attention it gets? Well, not if you're indifferent to being taken to the peak of gustatory pleasure by the simplest ingredients that nature can provide; to stand grinning while swirls of spicy mint and sweet, nectary tamarind chutneys spiral to your stomach to luxuriate there until it groans in concert with your brain, "No More!" If that sounds good to you, brother, you have come to the right page.

Papdis

These savory crackers are used in the preparation of a wide variety of chaats. While they can be bought from stores, homemade is always better—though it's only fair to warn you that they are tedious to prepare for a large, hungry family or for the neighborhood bowling league, as the dough has to be painstakingly hand rolled.

White flour	250 g/1¼ cups
Cumin seeds/jeera	3 g/½ tsp
Melted ghee	20 g/1 tbsp
Salt	a pinch
Carom seeds/ajwain (optional)	a pinch
Cold water for kneading	50 ml/¼ cup
Ghee	to deep fry

Sift the salt and flour together. Add the cumin and carom seeds. Add the melted ghee and work the flour with your fingers achieving a crumbly texture. Add enough of the cold water and knead until it becomes a stiff dough.

On a flat surface, roll the dough to the thickness of a nickel. Use a round cutter or a shot glass to cut out one inch diameter discs. Prick each disc a couple of times with a fork to prevent them from puffing up and ensuring that they stay crisp. The remnants of the cutouts can be rerolled together.

Heat the ghee in a heavy bottomed pot. Fry the papdis at 130ºC/250ºF until they are golden brown on each side. Remove and drain on absorbent kitchen paper toweling. They can be stored in an airtight container for a couple of months.

Tip: Most Indian recipes use oils other than ghee in which to fry. This is due to its high cost, but frying in ghee results in a longer lasting crispness than does the use of other oils.

Tip: Frying the dough at a low temperature ensures that you will have a crisper final product.

Golgappa Puris

Whole wheat flour	100 g/½ cup
Semolina	100 g/½ cup
Melted ghee	20 g/1 tbsp
Cold water	20 ml/1 tbsp
Ghee	to deep fry

Mix together the flour and the semolina. Gently warm the ghee until it melts and add it to the flour. Knead with sufficient water to make a stiff dough. Use a damp cloth to cover the dough and rest it in a cool place for half an hour.

Roll the dough into long slim ropes and cut them into marble-sized pieces. With a rolling pin, roll out each ball into a thin circle of an inch – to an inch-and-a half in diameter. Being tiny, they will stick to the pin, but are easily pulled off. Slide these discs into the hot ghee and turn them over until they puff up and are golden on each side. Remove and drain excess oil.

These can be stored in airtight containers for about three weeks.

What-Nots

Savory Gram Flour Vermicelli
Sev

Although sev is available in most Asian/Indian food stores, it is fun to make and very satisfying to create one's self at home. You will need a vermicelli press. It looks similar to a cookie press and is available at most Asian stores.

Bengal gram flour/Besan	200 g/1 cup
Rice flour	100 g/½ cup
Oil	20 ml/1 tbsp
Cumin seeds	a pinch
Carom seeds/ajwain	a pinch
Baking soda	a pinch
Chili powder	3 g/½ tsp
Turmeric	a pinch
Salt	to taste
Oil	to deep-fry

Sift the flour with the salt. Knead gently incorporating enough oil to form a crumb-like texture. Add the cumin seeds, carom seeds, soda, chilli, and turmeric. Knead, adding enough water to make a stiff dough.

Heat the oil in a fryer or in a heavy-bottomed pot.

Grease the vermicelli press. Squeeze the mixture directly into the hot oil.

With a long cooking fork, stir the vermicelli gently to prevent their sticking together. Fry over medium heat until crispy. Remove with a slotted spoon and drain on absorbent paper towels. These will keep for a month if stored in an airtight container.

Savory Semolina Hash

Rawa upma

When I first became vegetarian, I was a college student with big ambitions and little money. Many of those big ambitions have been realized, yet the money level ironically remains the same.

It being a pretty substantial meal, I often made a large pot of this easy-to-prepare and inexpensive dish. Filling and nourishing, the ingredients are readily available, and being truly tasty, it doesn't require a student's budget to appreciate it.

Semolina	200 g/1 cup
Oil	20 ml/1 tbsp
Mustard seeds	3 g/½ tsp
Cumin seeds	a pinch
Curry leaves	1 sprig
Onions, chopped	50 g/¼ cup
Ginger, shredded	5 g/1 tsp
Fresh chilis, chopped	5 g/1 tsp
Tomatoes, chopped	75 g/⅜ cup
Turmeric	5 g/1 tsp
Hot water	375 ml/1¾ cups (approximately)
Salt	to taste
Coriander leaves, chopped	5 g/1 tsp

Heat the oil in a heavy-bottomed pan and add the mustard, cumin, and curry leaves. When the seeds crackle, add the onions and stir them on low heat until they are golden. Add the ginger, fresh chilis, and tomatoes and cook on low heat until the tomatoes turn pulpy. Add the semolina, salt, and turmeric, stir a few times, add the hot water and simmer until the mixture is thick and the semolina has cooked through—about ten to twelve minutes Taste and adjust the salt, if required. Stir in the chopped coriander leaves and serve hot. If it's not yet complete, finish that term paper!

Savory Gram Flour and Yogurt Rolls
Khandvi

My mother liked to make tea-time an interesting affair. Although she was not particularly good with some of our main meals, her snacks were better by far than those of the commercial establishments so highly lauded by many.

The trip home from school always provided an exciting guessing game imagining what newest creation would be laid out at tea time. Khandvi, requiring a bit of patience and skill, were definitely the most sought after.

Besan	225 g/½ lb
Fresh chilis, stems removed	4
Ginger, peeled	5 g/1 tsp
Yogurt	300 ml/1½ cups
Water	100 ml/½ cup
Turmeric–	3 g/½ tsp
Salt	to taste
Oil	20 ml/1 tbsp
Mustard seeds	3 g/½ tsp
Dried chilis, finely chopped	2
Asafoetida	a pinch
Coconut, grated	5 g/1 tsp
Coriander leaves, chopped	5 g/1 tsp

Process the chilis with the ginger and a bit of water in a food processor to obtain a smooth paste. Whisk together the gram flour, ginger-chili paste, yogurt, water, turmeric, and salt to obtain a smooth batter that will coat the back of a spoon.

Simmer the batter over a low flame in a heavy-bottomed pot, stirring the entire time with a wooden spoon. When it thickens sufficiently to seem likely to turn into a solid mass—about twenty five minutes—and has a shiny surface, remove from heat. Liberally rub oil onto a sheet of stainless steel, the back of a steel serving tray, or a pastry marble. While the cooked mixture is still warm, spread it with a palette knife as thinly as possible. Use a knife to score the batter into inch-wide strips. Lift one end of the now cooled and firm batter and roll up the strip toward the other end. Roll the rest of the strips in the same manner.

Heat 1 tbsp of oil in a heavy-bottomed pan and add the mustard seeds. When they crackle add the dried chilis and asafoetida. Swirl the oil over the flame for a few seconds and then pour it as evenly as possible over the prepared khandvi rolls that have been set side by side on a serving dish. Sprinkle the rolls with grated coconut and coriander leaves and serve warm or at room temperature.

Sambhar

Served all over southern India, this is a traditional vegetable and spice gravy having numerous variations. The vegetables or the spices can be altered to suit the occasion or to complement other dishes that will be served with it during the meal. Drumsticks are vegetables that are local to South India and are difficult to find in the U.S. While certainly not traditional to do so, drumstick can be omitted without endangering the result.

I have included the traditional recipe for the spice powder although there are many commercial spice mixes available that can be used as a substitute. Although the recipe sounds tedious and time consuming, it really isn't. It gets easier each time and since our brethren in the south eat it at almost every meal, they can whip it up in no time flat.

For the sambhar spice powder

Coriander seeds	a pinch
Dried red chillies	3
Black peppercorns	a pinch
Cumin seeds	a pinch
Fenugreek seeds	a pinch
Mustard seeds	a pinch
Split Bengal gram/Chana dal	a pinch
Poppy seeds	a pinch
Grated coconut	5 g/1 tsp
Cinnamon stick	1 piece, about 2–3 inches in length
Curry leaves	one sprig

For the Gravy

Drumstick, cut inch-long sticks	75 g/⅓ cup
Shallots peeled	50 g/¼ cup
Potatoes peeled, cut into inch-long sticks of pinky finger thickness	50 g/¼ cup
Daikon, peeled and cut into 1-inch cubes	50 g/¼ cup

Pumpkin peeled and cut into 1-inch cubes	75 g/⅓ cup
Fresh chillies cut in half lengthwise	2
Tuvar dal	150 g/¾ cup
Sambhar powder	15 g/1 tbsp
Turmeric	5 g/1 tsp
Tamarind pulp	15 g/1 tbsp
Salt	to taste
Chopped coriander leaves	5 g/1 tsp

For the Tempering

Oil	10 ml/2 tsp
Mustard seeds	a pinch
Asafoetida powder	a pinch
Cumin seeds	a pinch
Dried red chillies	2
Curry leaves	a sprig

Roast all the ingredients for the powder individually and grind them together to obtain a fine powder. Reserve

Boil ½ liter/2½ cups of water with the turmeric, salt, fresh chillies, tamarind pulp, sambhar spice powder, lentils, and all the vegetables. Simmer for twenty minutes until the vegetables are almost done and the gravy has begun to thicken.

Separately heat the oil and add the ingredients for the tempering. When the seeds splutter, swirl them around in the hot oil a couple of times and pour this over the stewed vegetables. Stir the stew for a couple of minutes until the seasonings have blended, taste and adjust the seasoning, if required. Sprinkle on the coriander leaves and serve hot.

Tip: Readymade sambhar powder is available prepackaged in many Indian provision stores.

Desserts

Sweets play an extremely important role in Indian culture. They are used on many important occasions, which may include the announcement of births, festivals, during religious ceremonies, and at weddings. Sweets are rarely eaten without first being offered to the gods. They are placed at the altar in the house, blessings are invoked, and they are then distributed.

A love of sweets has left the nation reeling under twin epidemics of obesity and diabetes—but of course this has done little to deter those who put the pleasures of the palate above health warnings. We have faith that one day a scientific breakthrough will proclaim that all that one has feared about obesity, bad cholesterol, and overeating was merely propaganda promoted by legions of stick-thin runway models.

Although this national cuisine possesses the greatest number of desserts in terms of variety, tastes, and textures, they have rarely crossed over into other cuisines due to the staggering quantities of sugar they require.

Beside labor, which is rather plentiful in India, sugar is also among the cheapest ingredients one can use. Early sweets-makers realized that the more sugar they put into a recipe, the more they could reduce other, costlier ingredients. Sugar is a substance pleasing to most palates and in the summary course of evolution an entire nation became addicted to a multitude of overly sweet desserts.

Some sweets that are prepared by poaching or steeping in sugar syrup were intended to be prepared that way. For the remainder, I have stuck to the original recipes, those created before the commercial sweets preparation industry became such a dominant force in India. Sugar, being the cheapest ingredient on the list, commercial sweets makers increase the amount of sugar to keep their cost low because sweets are sold by weight.

Cardamom And Saffron-Fragranced Cheese Dumplings

Rajbhog

The rajbhog is a Bengali dessert thought to be fit for a king. Innovated a little after Rosogulla (see page 202) had been created, this sweet occupies a very important position in the hierarchy of Bengali sweetdom.

Dumplings

Whole milk	1 liter/1 quart
Lemon juice	40 ml/2 tbsp

Stuffing

Whole milk	150 ml/¾ cup
Sugar	20 g/1 tbsp
Toasted shelled pistachios (dry roast them in a hot pan as one would do for spices)	30 g/2 tbsp
Crushed green cardamom pods, with husks	5

For the Syrup

Water	one liter/1 quart (approximately)
Sugar	350 g/1 ¾ cup
Cornstarch	10 g/2 tsp
Saffron strands	a pinch
Rosewater (optional)	3 ml/½ tsp

To make the dumplings

Bring the milk to a boil and add the lemon juice, when the milk curdles, almost immediately, remove from heat. Pour the curdled milk solids into a damp cheesecloth, knot the opposite corners, run it under cold tap water for ten minutes and then hang it in a cool place for about half an hour to allow excess liquid to drain off.

To make the stuffing mixture

Boil the milk and sugar together until the milk is reduced to half. Add the cardamom and pistachios and simmer for an hour, reducing it further, until the mixture thickens to the consistency of a thick porridge

To make the syrup

Boil the sugar and water together until the sugar dissolves. Add the saffron strands.

Divide the dumpling mixture and hand-roll it into golf ball-sized balls. Flatten them in your palm and place about half a teaspoon of the stuffing into each dumpling. Form it into a ball again, with the stuffing in the middle, and immerse them in the boiling sugar syrup. Boil these for about twenty minutes until they rise to the surface and have a soft, spongy texture.

After cooking the dumplings, whisk the cornstarch in about 25 ml/2 tbsp of water and add it to the boiling syrup. Stir gently over a low flame until the mixture thickens.

Remove from the heat and let the dumplings and the syrup cool. Chill. Drizzle on rosewater just before serving for those who prefer.

Rasgulla

Anyone who goes to Kolkatta (previously Calcutta) should not return without completing a unique pilgrimage. Homage should be paid to a most famous Bengali confection, the "Roshogulla." The "Roshogulla" or "rasgulla" has a time-honored altar—the sweet shop of K.C. Das and Son—which has several braches spread throughout the city—from the congested Baghbazar to seedy Ripon street.

K.C Das and Sons, now global, could not have managed this fame were it not for the innovation and creativity of a noble ancestor named Nobin Chandra Das.

Nobin Chandra Das was born in 1846 into a family that controlled the sugar industry in Bengal at that time. With the passage of time, declining family fortune denied young Das the comfort and ease his predecessors had enjoyed.

Nobin Chandra Das lost his father three months before his birth. As formal education could not be provided, given the limited family resources, he set up a sweet shop in 1864 in Jorsanko, Kolkatta. That shop failed.

Not one to give up, he pursued a second similar venture in 1866 in Baghbazar, Kolkatta. This shop did moderately well. Hoping to do something more worthwhile in his life, one that would leave an indelible mark, the young Nobin conceived of the rasgulla in 1868. During the time when the "Sandesh," a dry, reduced-milk cheese, reigned supreme in Bengal, the syrupy rasgulla stood out in stark contrast.

As time went by, the fame and popularity of the sweet grew and grew. When his son Krishna took over, Krishna expanded the family business and pioneered a number of innovations in the field of confectionery such as "Rasmalai" and the first canned desserts in the country. Today the K.C. Das brand is a very important part of the Bengali culture.

Soft cottage cheese /channa (recipe below)	500 g/1.1 lb
Corn starch–	15 g/1 tbsp
Castor Sugar or cane sugar	20 g/1 tbsp

For the Syrup

Sugar	1 kg/2.2 lbs
Water	3 liters/3 quarts
Rose Water	50 ml/¼ cup
Milk	10 ml/2 tsp

Squeeze the water out of the channa (soft cottage cheese is called channa) until it is completely dry. Knead the channa and sugar to a smooth paste and until all the sugar has been dissolved. Add the cornstarch and continue kneading until smooth. Form the kneaded paste into marble-sized balls and set aside. Cover with a damp cloth.

For the Sugar Syrup

Bring the sugar and water to a boil and add the milk. The milk will curdle and rise to the top and will also produce scum. Spoon the curdled milk and scum out of the syrup. Reduce the heat to a simmer, and add the dumplings. They will rise to the top when done. Taking care to ensure that the sugar syrup does not thicken by reducing the heat as and when necessary, let the rasgollas simmer for twenty minutes. Serve chilled.

Sweetened Sugar-Soaked Cardamom Pancakes

Malpoa

This is a thing that anyone who eats sweets will love! With no effort at all I could eat my way through an entire afternoon's output in ten minutes flat. Although Indians love sweets, they make very few of them at home, relying on the neighborhood shop to provide their desserts. Should you have an Indian-themed potluck dinner and a guest arrives with store-bought dessert, they should not be faulted for laziness, but heralded as one who knows the custom.

I have travelled through much of India, eating my way through every sweet shop I could find, much to the delight of their owners, in search of the perfect malpoa. My quest achieved its end when I met Ejaazda. He was a wrinkled old man—really—he resembled the mummified remains of King Tut. Ejaazda ran a tea stall on the way to Digha in West Bengal. He was a sorcerer of malpoas. His malpoas were so soft and silky they would swirl through one's mouth to disappear down one's throat like magic. At first he, of course, refused to part with his ancestral recipe. I interrupted my travels to stay there for fifteen days. Finally, after much being together and thousands (well, not really) of malpoas, and a few well-considered gifts—a saree for his wife, movie tickets for the family, an earthen pot for his home, and season tickets to the cricket matches, he relented. And, here, at only the mere price of this book, and not having first to engorge yourself with thousands of malpoas, you now will discover what I learned:

For the Sugar Syrup

Sugar	250 g/½ lb
Water	120 ml/⅔ cup
Green cardamom	4 pods
Juice of one lime	

For the Batter

White flour	250 g/½ lb
Ghee	20 g/1 tbsp
Oil	20 g/1 tbsp
Whole milk	250 ml/1 ¼ cup

Fennel seeds	5 g/1 tsp
Cardamom pods, crushed, including the husk	4
Ghee for frying	150 g/¾ cup

Boil together for a few minutes, all the ingredients for the syrup. Set it aside to cool.

For the batter, mix together the flour, ghee and oil. Add the milk slowly and blend it to a smooth batter. Add the fennel seeds and crushed cardamom pods. Mix well and rest for ten minutes.

In a flat-bottomed frying pan, heat the ghee to frying temperature. Ghee will support higher frying temperatures than other oils as the milk solids that would burn if it were still butter have been removed. Spoon a dollop of the mixture into the ghee to achieve a diameter of 4″ and fry, turning, until golden on both sides and the edges become crispy and curl up. Immerse them in the sugar syrup to sit for at least an hour to absorb the syrup. Gently warm the malpoas before serving. Served With vanilla ice cream, it's a wonder they are legal.

Sweetened Broken Wheat

Lapsi

This dessert is simple and easy to prepare. The consistency is akin to thickened porridge and it is considered both healthy and nutritious. Should you choose to, replace the oil with ghee which is used to make this recipe vegan-friendly.

Dahliya is available at most Indian provision stores

Broken wheat/Dahliya	200 g/1 cup
Oil	40 ml/2 tbsp
Sugar	100 g/½ cup
Raisins	10 g/2 tsp
Cashew nuts, broken	20 g/1 tbsp
Pistachios, shelled, whole or crushed	10 g/2 tsp
Cardamom powder	5 g/1 tsp
Hot water	approximately 500 ml/½ quart

Heat the oil and add the cashew nuts. Stir for a minute and add the raisins. Using a slotted spoon, remove the fruit and nuts when the cashews are golden and the raisins have puffed up. Set aside on paper to drain.

Reheat the same oil and fry the dahliya until it is golden. Add the sugar and when it has melted, add the hot water and reduce the flame to a simmer. Stir occasionally until all the water has been absorbed and the wheat is tender. If the wheat is not tender enough, you can add more water if necessary. Add the cardamom powder, fruits and nuts and taste. Serve warm.

Eggless Cashew Nut and Pistachio Ice Cream

Kaju-Pista Kulfi

This is a modern adaptation of traditional ice cream. Enormously opulent banquets were often laid out for the emperors. Runners were sent above the snow line to bring back enough ice to keep the emperor and his entourage cool while the sun god ensured that the rest of the nation sweltered.

The emperor in his good-natured benevolence would, of course, not offend the sensibilities of his vegetarian guests and neither did he deny them the pleasures of cooling "flavored ice" rather than ice cream that contained eggs. The royal chefs kept huge wooden ice cream churns moving with masses of exotic, egg-free, ice creams. This is one of their basic recipes. You may alter the flavor to suit your taste.

Unsalted cashew nuts, crushed	50 g/¼ cup
Unsalted pistachios, shelled, crushed	20 g/1 tbsp
Whole milk	1 liter/1 quart
Condensed milk	375 g/1 ½ cups
Heavy cream, lightly whipped to soft peaks	250 ml/¼ quart
White bread crumbs, crumbled fresh	20 g/1 tbsp

Gently stir together the milk and the breadcrumbs (which add a little body). Add the condensed milk and stir until it has been incorporated into the milk. Stir in the cream and the nuts. Taste and adjust sweetness by adding sugar, if necessary.

Pour the mixture into an ice cream maker and churn to get a smooth, creamy ice cream. Serve frozen.

Lotus Seed Pudding (or) No Lotus Seed Pudding— the U.S. Version

Phool Makhane ki Kheer

Lotus seeds /phool makhana (*can be omitted as they are difficult to find in the U.S.*)	200 g/1 cup
Milk	800 ml/4 cups
Sugar	150 g/¾ cup
Green cardamom	4 pods
Fennel seeds	a pinch
Ginger, grated	a pinch
Nutmeg, grated	a pinch
Cashew nuts, chopped	10 g/2 tsp
Raisins	10 g/2 tsp

Roast the lotus seeds (or not) in a dry, hot pan for about ten minutes over medium heat until they appear golden and crisp.

Separately bring the milk to a boil in a pot and simmer it gently along with the cardamom and fennel until it has reduced to half of its original volume. Add the sugar and ginger and bring it to a boil. Remove from heat. Add the lotus seeds and set aside to cool.

Stir in the nutmeg, cashew nuts and raisins and refrigerate. Serve chilled.

Sweetened Dried Fruits

Shufta

This Kashmiri dessert traditionally ended many royal banquets. As many find it to be cloyingly sweet, it can be adjusted to suit individual tastes.

This recipe is much enjoyed in the northern parts of the country where the winters can be particularly cold. This sugary preparation helps to generate a goodly amount of body heat.

Home-made paneer cubes	150 g/¾ cup
Ghee	40 g/2 tbsp
Raisins	40 g/2 tbsp
Dried pitted dates, halved	40 g/2 tbsp
Sultanas	40 g/2 tbsp
Cashew nuts	50 g/¼ cup
Pistachios, shelled	40 g/2 tbsp
Green cardamom	5 pods
Cinnamon stick	1 piece, about 2–3 inches in length
Sugar	200 g/1 cup
Saffron	a few strands
Kewra Water /screw pine essence (optional)	a dash

Heat the ghee in a heavy-bottomed pot and gently fry the paneer cubes until they are golden. Remove with a slotted spoon and set aside in a strainer to drain.

In the same pan, reheat the remaining ghee and add the nuts, dried fruits, and spices. When they begin to turn golden, remove them from the pan and reserve.

Place the sugar in a pot with 2 ½ cups/500 ml water and simmer for twenty minutes, until the liquid thickens sufficiently to coat a spoon. Add the fried ingredients and the saffron strands and simmer until the liquid thickens further, about ten minutes, coating the fruit and candying them in the process. Remove from heat, add a dash of the kewra water, if desired. Stir and serve warm.

Jalebis

Jalebis are a popular dessert in the north of India. A legend has it that the invading Mughal army brought jalebis to India in the fifteenth century, CE—but, in fact, there are mentions of Jalebis in the Vedas and the Sushrut-Samitha, a medical text written between the 4th and the 2nd centuries, BCE.

White flour	60 g/4 tbsp
Gram flour/besan	40 g/2 tbsp
Yogurt	20 g/1 tbsp

Oil	20 ml/1 tbsp
Sugar	100 g/½ cup
Water	50 ml/¼ cup
Juice of half a lemon	
Ghee	½ inch in pan for frying
Saffron	a few strands
Pistachio nuts, crushed	5 g/1 tsp

Sift the white flour and gram flour together. Warm the oil slightly and add it to the flour. Mix it into the flour and crumble it with your fingers. Add the yogurt and stir well. Add sufficient water to bring the mixture to a batter of pouring consistency. Set aside in a cool place (a refrigerator is too cool) to ferment for 24 hours.

Mix the sugar and water in a pot and bring it to a boil. Stir occasionally, simmering until the syrup is thick enough to coat the spoon. Add the lemon juice. Put the saffron strands into the still-hot liquid.

In a shallow pan melt the ghee and reduce the heat to moderate. Place the batter in a piping bag having a very fine nozzle. Pipe the batter directly into the hot ghee in a continuous spiral from the center out to about 4" in diameter. Fry and turn. Remove with a slotted spoon when both sides are golden. Place the fried jalebis directly into the sugar syrup. Allow them to soak in the syrup for a few minutes. Remove with a slotted spoon and serve garnished with chopped pistachio nuts.

Pulipithe

Pithes, of which pulipithe is one variety, are a traditional form of sweets. They come in a number of shapes and forms. As Indians have many options when it comes to types of sweeteners, there have been numerous experiments that coax out even greater variety. "Khejurgur" (a type of palm sugar extracted from the date palm) is considered best to sweeten this dish. It is a seasonal product available only in the eastern state of Bengal. If you can obtain Khejurgur, wonderful! If not, regular sugar works

While our family stayed in Mumbai, my mother-in-law went to extraordinary lengths to ensure that she obtained a steady stream of khejurgur with which to sweeten her desserts. She coaxed and bullied people, called in favors, threatened my father-in-law with only he knows what, and threw entertaining tantrums just to ensure that she got the product hand-carried from Bengal. With it, she created her magic:

Semolina	225 g/½ lb
Coconut, finely grated	150 g/¾ cup
Sugar	80 g/4 tbsp
Whole milk	900 ml/4½ cups
Palm/cane sugar	120 g/⅔ cup
Green cardamom, ground whole	3 pods
Salt	a pinch

Coarsely crush the palm sugar with a mortar and pestle. Heat the palm sugar and the coconut together on low heat. Stir continuously until the mixture is thick with a sheen and of a sticky consistency. Spread this mixture out on a flat tray to cool, allowing it to find its own depth.

Boil the semolina in 250 ml/1 ¼ cup of water. Simmer for fifteen minutes until the water has been absorbed. If the mixture is lumpy, whisk it a bit and continue to cook until it is smooth. Remove from heat and allow it to cool. Roll in the hands into marble-sized balls.

Flatten each ball in the palm of your hand. Put a little coconut filling into the center and close the semolina mixture around it, rolling it to form tapering cylinders. When all have been shaped, set them aside to rest for ten minutes. Bring the milk to a boil and reduce the heat, simmering until a quarter of the milk has evaporated. Add the sugar and stir until it has dissolved. Remove from heat. Sprinkle on the powdered cardamom and serve warm or at room temperature.

Stuffed Sweet Pancakes
Patishapta

Filling

Coconut, grated	350 g/1 ¾ cup
Sugar	250 g/1 ¼ cup
Cinnamon stick	1 piece, about 2–3 inches in length

| Salt | 3 g/½ tsp |
| Green cardamom, ground whole | 2 pods |

Pancakes

White flour	225 g/½ lb
Ghee	40 g/2 tbsp
Water	250 ml/1 ¼ cup
Sugar	20 g/1 tbsp

For the filling, cook all the ingredients together over low heat. Stir often to avoid the mixture sticking to the bottom. After ten minutes, it should be sufficiently cooked and thick. Remove from heat. Hand roll into twelve or so equally long cylinders of about 1 inch and set aside.

For the pancakes, mix together the flour and half of the ghee. Add most of the water and all of the sugar and whisk together to form a batter of coating consistency. (Add additional water as needed to reach the proper consistency for pancake batter.) Heat a non-stick pan and melt a little bit of ghee.

Pour a spoonful of the batter in the pan and swirl it around until a thin layer covers the bottom of the pan. Cook for thirty seconds and lift up the edges with a spatula. to see if they are done.

Lay a pancake flat on a work space and place a cylinder of the filling in the center and fold the pancake over it, wrapping the filling within the pancake like a burrito. Continue similarly until all the stuffing and the pancakes have been used.

Tip: The pancake can be folded in any of a variety of ways. They can be rolled into cylinders, folded into squares or triangles, or the filling can be sandwiched between two flat pancakes.

Wheat Flour And Rock Sugar Dumplings
Choorma ladoos

Cane sugar	100 g/½ cup
Wheat flour	300 g/1 ½ cup
Rock candy, using additional cane sugar is okay if rock candy is not available	70 g/⅓ cup

Ghee	300 g/1 ½ cup
Pistachio nuts, chopped	10 g/2 tsp
Almonds, chopped	10 g/2 tsp
Raisins	5 g/1 tsp
Salt	a pinch
Green cardamom pods, powdered	a pinch
Milk	40 ml/2 tbsp
Cloves, powdered	a pinch

Grind the table sugar and rock sugar together to a fine powder in a food processor or using a mortar and pestle. Reserve.

Mix about fifteen grams/one tablespoon of the ghee into the flour and knead well with your fingers to get dough of crumbly texture. Add the milk and knead to a stiff dough. Divide this mixture into marble-sized balls.

Heat 200 g/1 cup of the ghee in a pan and fry the balls over medium heat until they are golden. Remove with a slotted spoon and drain on absorbent kitchen paper toweling. Set them aside to cool. When cooled, process them to a fine powder in a food processor.

Mix this powder with the ground sugars, nuts, raisins, cardamom powder, clove powder, and about 100gm/½ cup of ghee, forming them into round dumplings of an inch and a half in diameter. These can be stored in an airtight container for up to a month.

Sweet Semolina Dumplings

Rawa Ladoo

Semolina	200 g/1 cup
Ghee	50 g/¼ cup
Sugar	50 g/¼ cup
Cardamom powder	10 g/2 tsp
Raisins	20 g/1 tbsp
Salt	a pinch

Place the ghee in a pot and warm it gently.

In a separate dry pan, toast the semolina while stirring until it is evenly golden. Remove from the heat, add the sugar, and stir well until the sugar is mostly melted (do not overheat to the point of candying) and evenly mixed.

Add the semolina mixture to the warm ghee along with the cardamom powder, raisins and salt. Mix well.

Form the mixture into golf ball-sized balls while it is still warm. These dumplings are served at room temperature.

A large batch can be made as they keep well. Stored in an airtight container they will keep for a couple of weeks to be enjoyed at will.

Pineapple Halwa
Ananas Halwa

Pineapple, chopped, canned or fresh	150 g/¾ cup
Green cardamom	3 pods
Fennel seeds	5 g/1 tsp
Cashew nuts, chopped	5 g/1 tsp
Raisins	5 g/1 tsp
Sliced almonds	5 g/1 tsp
Pistachios, crushed	5 g/1 tsp
Sugar	40 g/2 tbsp
Ghee	10 g/2 tsp
Semolina	20 g/1 tbsp

Heat the ghee in a heavy-bottomed pot and add the cardamom and fennel seeds. When the seeds splutter, add the chopped pineapple and stir rapidly over high heat. After two minutes, when the pineapple chunks turn golden, add the sugar, nuts, raisins, and semolina. Reduce the heat to a simmer for about five minutes, stirring occasionally to prevent sticking. The dish will thicken, but be sure not to overcook. The pineapple should remain chunky though the semolina is cooked through. Serve warm.

Traditional Indian Carrot Dessert
Gajar ka Halwa

Carrots, peeled and grated	300 g/1 ½ cup
Whole milk	300 ml/1 ½ cup
Condensed milk	100 g/½ cup
Sugar	70 g/⅓ cup
Cardamom powder	3 g/½ tsp
Cashew nuts, broken	10 g/2 tsp
Raisins	10 g/2 tsp
Pistachios, crushed	5 g/1 tsp
Ghee	20 g/1 tbsp
Salt	a pinch

Heat the ghee in a pan. Add the raisins. When they puff up, add the grated carrots, stirring rapidly. Cook for about five minutes until the carrots turn soft and become a darker shade.

Add the whole milk, simmering and stirring regularly as the milk reduces to a third of its original volume. Add the cashew nuts, pistachios, and condensed milk (Nestle and Carnation are found in India). The mixture will thicken as most of the moisture will be absorbed or have been expended as steam and the milk will coat the carrots.

Add the sugar (less, if you like), a pinch of salt, and the cardamom powder. Stir, mixing well. Taste and adjust the sugar as required. Serve warm.

Drinks

Rose syrup
Gulab ki Shikanji

This is an absolutely brilliant summer cooler. Although there are a several good commercial varieties available, I sometimes like to steep my own syrup and do away with the chemical colors and additives. Although the color may not be as rich as those available in the market, the fragrance and flavor more than make up for it.

I prefer to use petals of a single color rather than to mix them. Although you may find this to sound slightly balmy, I assure you that each differently colored rose has its own unique fragrance and flavor.

The kewra essence, sometimes referred to as orris water or screw pine essence, is available at many Indian provision stores.

Rose petals	200 g/1 cup packed tightly
Sugar	1 kg/5 cups
Rose water	20 ml/1 tbsp
Kewra water/screw pine essence (optional)–	5 ml/1 tsp

Mix the rose petals with about 200 g/1 cup of sugar and leave them covered in a cool place for two days. It will appear frothy at the top, from mild fermentation

Gently simmer the remaining sugar with about three liters/three quarts of water for an hour to form a thick sugar syrup. Add the rose petals and the liquid resultant from the fermentation. Simmer for about an hour longer, to ensure that all the fragrance and flavor of the roses has been released. Add the rose water and screw pine essence (if desired). Remove from the heat when the liquid is quite thick. Strain. Cool the liquor and dilute it to taste with iced water or soda before serving.

Tip: Kewra water adds an astringent touch to the sweetness

Sweetened Yogurt and Cardamom Drink
Lassi

Yogurt	400 g/2 cups
Green cardamom	5 pods
Sugar	75 g/⅓ cup
Rose water (optional)	10 ml/2 tsp

Grind the cardamom pods with half the sugar in a food processor or mortar and pestle to obtain a fine powder. Pass this through a sieve and discard the residual.

Whisk the yogurt in a bowl with the cardamom powder, sugar, rose water (if desired), and 100 ml/½ cup of water. Taste and adjust the sweetness, if required. Refrigerate and serve chilled.

Honey and Lemon Cooler
Nimbu pani

Honey	150 g/¾ cup
Lemons	4
Mint leaves, chopped	5 g/1 tsp

Simmer 700 ml/3 ½ cups of water with the honey. Stir until the honey is melted. Remove from heat and set aside to cool.

Add the lemon juice and add the mint leaves and mix them in. Serve over ice or refrigerate until chilled.

Rose Petal Tea
Gulabi Chai

Rose petal tea? Hey! I ask again, "Rose petal tea?!"

Well, in fairness, I did hear you the first time and chose to ignore it. But, you had to question it again! Yeah! Really! Rose petal tea!

It ain't pansy petal tea! It is, in fact, a wonderfully fragrant, totally refreshing drink. I take mine splashed over ice cubes, pardner!

Rose petals	20 g/1 tbsp
Fennel seeds	10 g/2 tsp
Green cardamom	2 pods
Cinnamon stick	1 piece, about 2–3 inches in length
Honey	60 g/3 tbsp
Lemon juice	5 ml/1 tsp
Shredded mint leaves	a few leaves

Lightly roast the fennel seeds in a pan or on a griddle plate. Bring them to a boil with rose petals, cardamom, cinnamon, and 500 ml/2½ cups of water. Reduce the heat and simmer until the liquid has reduced to half the original quantity.

Pour the honey, mint and lemon juice into glasses and strain the liquid into them. Stir until the honey dissolves and serve warm or chilled.

Indian Spiced Tea (The Real Stuff)

Garam masala chai

A spiced tea that is very different from the 'masala chai' that people have come to expect.

Green cardamom	10 pods
Cinnamon sticks	2 pieces, about 2–3 inches in length
Cloves	6 buds
Fennel seeds	a pinch
Cumin seeds	a pinch
Honey	60 g/3 tbsp

Individually roast the cardamom, cinnamon, cloves, fennel and cumin until they begin to change color. Transfer them to a pot and simmer them in 500 ml/2½ cups of water for about twenty minutes. Remove from the heat and strain the tea, discarding the spices. Stir in the honey until it melts and serve warm.

Papaya, Ginger and Coconut Milk Cooler

Narkol pepeyer rosha

Peeled and cleaned ripe papaya	400 g/2 cups
Coconut milk	500 ml/2 ½ cups
Peeled and chopped ginger	10 g/2 tsp
Palm sugar	50 g/¼ cup
Crushed black pepper	a pinch
Chopped mint leaves	5 g/1 tsp

In a food processor, blend together the papaya, coconut milk, ginger, palm sugar and black pepper to get a smooth juice. Stir in the chopped mint and serve chilled.

Hints and Kinks

If you've gotten this far in the book you deserve a special reward. Following are some "Oh Boy! What do I do now?" bailouts. These are just a few of the deep, dark secrets held by chefs, that only some of you will have found elsewhere.

If you've made your dish too hot, a bit of cooling can be had by adding a pinch of sugar or a chopped tomato, or both, and cooking the dish down to incorporate the tomato. If you want to pretty much hide the tomato being there at all, first blanch and then skin the tomato--a good thing to do in most instances, anyway. Doing this will eliminate the telltale tomato skin chards that no one likes anyway—too crunchy.

If you burn a pot of rice, remove it from the heat and place a couple of slices of white bread flat on top of the rice while it's hot and steaming. This will help to absorb the burned flavor. If this doesn't help, then it's too burned. This, from an ancient bit of Indian learning—some things are beyond repair.

Oversalted a gravy? This is why most of my recipes say "salt to taste." One person's half-teaspoon is another's "pass the water bucket." To fix this, peel and add a potato (maybe not a huge Idaho) to the gravy. Boil it until it's cooked to tender and discard it before serving the dish. (Actually, you may be frugal, taste the potato, and, if it has not taken up too much of the salt, include it with the dish as it will have been flavored nicely by the gravy.)

Also good for oversalting is a squirt of lemon juice or some chopped tomato cooked to a pulp (see about the skins above).

Need to add chopped dried fruits and/or nuts to a recipe? Chill them in a refrigerator for a few hours. They will be much easier to chop if chilled first.

Need to measure out some honey? First spray the inside of your measuring spoon or cup with a coating of oil, using Pam or its equivalent. No oil spray? Soak a paper towel with oil and wipe it on—messy, but effective.

Are your stored potatos sprouting? To prevent this, keep an apple among them.

A toothbrush for the kitchen does a wonderful job cleaning such items as graters, micro-scrapers and planes, and garlic presses. Use a new one, others may impart a minty flavor.

www.ingramcontent.com/pod-product-compliance
Lightning Source LLC
Chambersburg PA
CBHW080459110426
42742CB00017B/2936